MEMBERS - ONE OF

The 9th 'Christ and the Cosmos' Publicati

Παρακαλω ουν υμας, αδελφοι, δια των οικτιρμων του θεου παραστησαι τα σωματα υμων θυσιαν ζωσαν αγιαν ευαρεστον τω θεο, την λογικην λατρειαν υμων. Και μη συσχηματιζεσθε τω αιωνι τουτω, αλλα μεταμορφουσθε τη ανακαινωσει του νοος εις το δοκιμαζειν υμας τι το θελημα του θεου, το αγαθον και ευαρεστον και τελειον.

ΠΡΟΣ ΡΩΜΑΙΟΥΣ, 12, 1-2.

Therefore I appeal to you brethren, through the mercies of God, to present your bodies as a living sacrifice, holy and acceptable to God, which is your spiritual worship. Do not be conformed to this age but be transformed by the renewal of your mind, that you may prove what is the will of God, what is good, acceptable and perfect.
Romans 12, 1-2

Others in the series:
"Christ and the Cosmos" (Conference year 1987)
"Christ and the Cosmos: Volume II" (1989)
"Christ and the Cosmos: Volume III" (1990)
"Christ and the Cosmos: Mission and Complexity" (1991)
"Christ and the Cosmos: Interpreting the Cosmos" 91992)
"Christ and the Cosmos: Being Human in a Cosmic Context" (1993)
"Christ and the Cosmos: Being Responsible in a Cosmic Context" (1994)
and
Taking the Initiative: Introductions and Extracts from the 'Christ and the Cosmos' Initiative writings (published 1993)

ISBN 0 9514482 9 3

MEMBERS - ONE OF ANOTHER

Volume IX in the "Christ and the Cosmos" Series

*Proceedings of the Conference held at Westminster College,
Oxford from 21st to 23rd April 1995.*

Edited by P.A. Beetham

1995 Conference Co-ordinator K.B. Everard

Published by: The Christ and the Cosmos Initiative and Westminster College

Copywright:©The Christ and the Cosmos Initiative - February 1996

Publication Team
Editor:
Rev. P.A. Beetham, B.A., B.Sc., Ph.D., C.Biol., M.I.Biol.

Sound Recording:
Mr. Rowland Budgen, M.Phil., B.Ed., F.I.M.L.S., M.I.Biol.

Copy Preparation:
Mrs. J. Beetham

Readers' comments and enquiries on this book or about the Initiative in general will be welcomed.

Please address any correspondence to The Editor at The Manse, School Road, Terrington St. John, Wisbech, Cambs. PE14 7SE (until 1st August 1996) or at Trinity Manse, Tower Road, Felixstowe, Suffolk. IP11 7PR (after 1st August 1996).

CONTENTS

 Page No.

Foreword 1
Biographical Notes on Lecturers 2
Synopsis of Lectures 7

Part One
Introduction to a Theme - Dr. K.B. Everard 12
Psychology versus religion
    and the case of Happiness - Dr. Michael Argyle 35
The Experience of Sadness - Dr. Neville Stewart 54
The Psycho-dynamics of Life and Worship -
    Rev. Dr. Bruce Reed 74
Jesus the Psychologist - The Rev. Prof. L.J. Francis 105
A Sermon - Rev. S. Roebuck 127

Part Two
Work - Mr. David C. Sutton 134
Children in the Family - Mrs. Linda Gow 137
Children at School - Mrs. Gwyneth Little 146
Clergy Personality - Rev. Prof. L.J. Francis 148
Youth - Dr. William K. Kay 151

Appendix
Meditation - Rev. Prof. L.J. Francis 156
Reading List 159
Consciousness and transcendental reality 161

Foreword

The 1995 Consultation extended the Christ and The Cosmos discussion into new areas. This followed logically from the 1993 meeting "Being Human in a Cosmic Context", Volume 7 which considered human knowledge, the workings of the human brain and mind, the functioning of society, aesthetic appreciation and the human spirit. Here we move on to consider mind and spirit in greater depth as we explored psychology in the light of Christian faith.

Our speakers addressed complimentary and contrasting topics and they used a wide variety of approaches. Indeed the range of methods and analytical processes seems bewildering when compared to those used by those engaged in the physical or life-sciences. The diversity found in these papers is much more reminiscent of the approach of theologians. In psychology as in theology the use of different methodologies and angles of approach is enormously productive.

Our enterprise is not a new one for we follow in the footsteps of many others such as Leslie Weatherhead and Frank Lake who have sought to use the insights and methods of psychology in the exercise of Christian pastoral care. This book like their work concerns both the individual and society and with the complex and inextricable relationship between them. We are indeed "Members One of Another".

The papers presented in this volume are the works of their authors rather than transcripts of the lectures given at the Consultation. In some cases the text and the lecture are very similar but in others the authors have reworked their material to make it more suitable for the printed page. I am grateful to all of the contributors. Thanks are also due to Mrs. Janet Beetham who typed the scripts for this volume.

Paul Beetham

Biographical Notes - 1995

Dr. K. B. Everard, M.A., B.Sc., D.Phil., F.R.S.A., F.I.P.D.
Bertie Everard gained a first in Natural Sciences at Magdalen College, Oxford and joined I.C.I Plastics Division as a research chemist in 1951. In 1966 he became the Division's (and in 1975 the Company's) Education and Training Manager, applying behavioural sciences to management and organisation development; his work is described in Professor Andrew Pettigrew's book "The Awakening Giant" (Blackwell 1985).
Retiring early in 1982 he has trained over 1000 headteachers and co-authored a best seller, "Effective School Management" (Paul Chapman 2e: 1990); he was a Visiting Professor of the Polytechnic of Central London and a Visiting Fellow of the University of London Institute of Education. His research on the problems of school management was published in "Developing Management in Schools" (Blackwell 1986). As a consultant in organisational behaviour he has worked for the U.R.C. (of which is an elder), the then D.E.S and D.H.S.S. and a Leicestershire school. A former Arthur Rank Lecturer at Luton Industrial College, he has been associated with the Christ and Cosmos Initiative since its inception.

Dr. Michael Argyle D.Sc., D.Litt., Hon.D.Sc.,Psych., Hon.F.B.Ps.S.
Michael Argyle has been teaching at Oxford for a long time, and carried out research into social skills, non-verbal communication, social relationships, the psychology of religion and the causes of happiness. He is now Emeritus Reader in Social Psychology at Oxford University, an Emeritus Fellow of Wolfson College, and Emeritus Professor at Oxford Brookes University. He has written about 25 books, including "The Psychology of Happiness" and "The Psychology of Interpersonal Behaviour" (5th edition 1994).
He has no religious credentials, but was once a Benedictine oblate, and is now an active member of the University Church.

Rev. Dr. Neville Stewart, M.A., B.Sc., Hon.D.D.
Neville Stewart has been married for 39 years, has 4 sons and 6 grandchildren. Originally an analytical/research chemist, he became a Methodist minister, spending 12 years in Circuit and 27 years as Head of Comprehensive Schools. He has been Director of two national organisations and worked as a management consultant/trainer. Recovered from 2 years of illness with severe ME and depression, he now works as a counsellor and meditation guide as part of a holistic approach to the recovery and maintenance of health = salvation.

Mr. David C. Sutton, B.Sc., A.R.C.S., M.B.A.
David Sutton started his working life as a chemistry graduate (Imperial College) in aerospace. After 12 years he left and studied full time for a Masters degree in Business Administration. In 1979 he successfully graduated and founded a management consultancy devoted to applying systems approaches to the resolution of complex general management problems.
David has unique experience in integrating the application of behavioural, scientific, sociotechnical and cybernetic approaches to business situations. He frequently works with senior executives on issues of strategic importance, providing services to decision makers and programme makers. He has worked in the U.K., Western Europe, U.S.A. and Africa, with all types of organisation, in all sectors, of all sizes. Apart from his commercial management development activities, David Sutton has also taught at degree and postgraduate level in a number of business schools..

Mrs. Linda Gow, B.Sc.Psych., M.A.(Appl.Psych), Post Grad. Dipl.(Family Therapy).
Linda Gow trained in Clinical Psychology in New Zealand in 1986 and has been practising in England since August 1987. She has worked within the Mental Health Services of the N.H.S. with both adults and children, individually, as couples and in family groups.

In 1990 she moved from London to Bristol where her husband spent 4 years studying theology in order to qualify for the ordained ministry in the Church of England. It was whilst in Bristol that she made a serious attempt to integrate her skills as a psychologist with her Christian Faith. This was mainly in the context of providing supervision to a Christian Counselling organisation and in contributions to an introductory course at her local church on the Christian Healing Ministry. She is also an active member of N.E.C.I.P. (Network of Christians in Psychology).

Dr. J.S. Lawes, B.Sc., M.Ed., Ph.D.
Jim Lawes took his first degree, in biology, at Durham. While teaching science and maths. in schools he became intrigued by the processes involved in understanding these subjects and took a degree in psychology of education including research on spatial and non-verbal abilities. Moving on he became a lecturer in education at Westminster College particularly concerned with the role of psychology in teaching. During his time at Westminster he investigated the part played by non-verbal communication in classrooms and based his Ph.D. thesis on this. After a career in teacher education which spanned the many changes in education and in teacher training he took early retirement.
He co-authored a book "Understanding Children" for students in African colleges and has contributed papers to professional journals. On a number of occasions he has been a visiting professor in the U.S.A. A life-long Methodist, he is an active member of Wesley Memorial Church in Oxford, and is married to a theologian.

Mrs. Gwyneth Little, B.A.
Lecturer Westminister College, Oxford and consultation steward.

Rev. Professor Leslie J. Francis, M.A., M.Sc., M.Th., B.D., Ph.D., F.B.Ps.S, F.C.P.
Leslie Francis studied theology at Oxford, Cambridge and Nottingham and psychology at Cambridge and London. He trained for ministry in

the Anglican church at Westcott House and was ordained in 1973. He has served in both stipendiary and non-stipendiary pastoral ministry. Currently he holds the D.J.James Chair of Pastoral Theology in the University of Wales, at Trinity College Carmarthen and St. David's University College Lampeter. His main research interests are in psychology of religion, religious education and the rural church. His books include "Youth in Transit" (1982), "Experience of Adulthood" (1982), "Young and Unemployed" (1984), "Teenagers and the Church" (1984), "Rural Anglicanism" (1985), "Partnership in Perspectives on Faith Development" (1992), "Christian Perspectives on Church Schools" (1993), "Critical Perspectives on Christian Education" (1994), "Teenage Religion and Values" (1994) and "Psychological Perspectives on Christian Ministry" (1995). He is also co-author of the "Teddy Horsley" series of books for 3-7 year olds.

Dr. William K. Kay, M.Ed., Ph.D
William Kay read English at Oxford and then taught in state schools for ten years. He took an M.Ed. in comparative education and then a Ph.D. in the same subject (looking at the teaching of religion in three cultural contexts): both these degrees at Reading University. In 1989 he took a Ph.D. in theology at Nottingham. He has been working as a Senior Research Fellow at the Centre for Theology and Education in Camarthen since the start of 1994.

Dr. John N. Hall, M.Sc., Ph.D., C.Psychol.,, F.B.Ps.S.
John Hall studied psychology at University College, Durham, before obtaining his post graduate degrees in clinical psychology at Leeds University. He worked in the N.H.S. at Norwich and Cardiff, and as a Research Fellow at Leeds University, before moving to Oxford in 1980. He is currently Professional Adviser in Clinical Psychology for Oxfordshire Health Authority, and Honorary Senior Lecturer in Clinical Psychology at Oxford University. He has recently completed a term as Consultant Adviser in Clinical Psychology to the Department of Health, and has written on a range of academic and professional

topics in the general area of clinical and health psychology, chronic disability and care.

Since he moved to Oxford he has taught pastoral psychology part-time at Wycliffe Hall theological college, and has been closely involved with the Oxford Christian Institute for Counselling, and with the recently formed national Network of Christians in Psychology. He is particularly concerned with exploring the pastoral relevance, in the local congregational setting, of the human and social sciences.

Rev. Dr. Bruce Reed, M.A., M.Litt., Th.L.

Bruce Reed is the President of the Grubb Institute which he was instrumental in founding in 1969 to contribute to the well-being and spirituality of society in a rapidly changing context, using the disciplines of systemics, psycho-analysis and theology. His work in Organisational Role Analysis with bishops, church leaders, and parish clergy on leadership roles, developed a systematic approach to the mission and work of the churches. His major conceptual writing, "The Dynamics of Religion" (1978) was further developed with colleagues in "The Parish Church" (1988) and in other papers. The Lambeth M.Litt. gave recognition of these contributions to the Church of England.

Rev. Stuart W. Roebuck, B.D., F.C.I.I.

Stuart Roebuck is a Methodist Minister, currently serving as Chaplain and Head of Religious Studies at Culford School in Suffolk. Before entering the ministry he had wide experience of industrial and commercial life in the Midlands and the north of England. He is a Trustee of the Christ and the Cosmos Initiative and from its inception to 1994 has edited the Christ and the Cosmos volumes and other reports. His other publications include "An Introduction to the Methodist Church and its Boarding Schools" (1985 - 2nd edition 1989), "Chapel Folk (1989), "And Finally - a Collection of some of Bill Gowland's Sermons" (1992), and with Dr. David Gowland "Never Call Retreat" (1990) and "Taking the Initiative" (1993).

Synopses of Session - 1995

Dr. K.B. Everard, M.A., B.Sc., D.Phil., F.R.S.A., F.I.P.D.
Introduction to the Theme
The most complex structure in the cosmos is probably the human brain, the organ that controls our behaviour, and on which the Holy Spirit is presumed to work. The behavioural sciences attempt to explain, interpret and characterise individual and collective behaviour, just at the physical sciences address the behaviour and characteristics of physical systems, and biological sciences of living systems.
In this session we shall establish some links, similarities and differences between the three branches of science and explore how the behavioural sciences contribute to our understanding of what it is to be human - "members one of another". By considering some applications, we shall see how these sciences can help to fulfil God's purpose for mankind as the Creation evolves.

Dr. Michael Argyle, D.S., D.Litt., Hon.D.Sc.Psych., Hon.F.B.Ps.S.
Psychology v. Religion and the Causes of Happiness
Bridging the gap between psychology and religion - the role of consciousness and ideas in behaviour, the nature and causes of beliefs, research on religious experience, the effects of religion on well-being and prosocial behaviour, the nature of love, the social evolution of religion.
Psychology's contribution to the sources of happiness - social relationships, social support and social skills training, work and job satisfaction, leisure - the source which is most easily controlled, and certain aspects of personality. Mood induction and the enhancement of happiness.
Can psychology be used to evaluate religion? Some kinds of religion which have negative effects. Rigid beliefs and inter-group conflict.

Rev. Dr. Neville Stewart, M.A., B.Sc., Hon.D.D.
The Experience of Sadness
A positive, experiential, holistic analysis of the why/what/how of sadness; how it can be a means of grace; with particular reference to the case study provided by the two men on a journey to Emmaus in chapter 24 of the Gospel according to St. Luke.

Mr. David C. Sutton, B.Sc., A.R.C.S., M.B.A.
Work
There is an increasing recognition in businesses of the relevance of "holistic" or "systems" approaches. Such approaches serve to counteract the tendency of people under stress and in complex situations to be increasingly narrow and simplistic in their viewpoints and fixed in their behaviours.
David will introduce his version of a "systems" perspective and use some exercises to give participants a feel for the ways managerial tools help people to get to grips with the "big picture" for their situations. It is hoped that this will stimulate discussions on the correspondence between their "managerial" ideas and religious doctrines relevant to "Being Human in a Cosmic Context".

Mrs. Linda Gow, B.Sc.Psych., M.A.(Appl.Psych), Post Grad.Dipl.(Family Therapy)
Children in the Family
1. Briefly explain my theoretical model of practice (drawing on psychology and biblical guidelines)
2. Outline the Family Life Cycle (from the child's perspective) from birth to adulthood.
3. Look at when unexpected/undesirable life events impinge upon development, e.g. premature death, separation/divorce, violence, abuse.
4. Discuss: how might having a Christian Faith make a difference to the way in which we manage family life.

5. Discuss: what should our response be to those amongst us experiencing undesirable/unexpected life events.
To facilitate 4 and 5 a case scenario may be provided.

Dr. J.S. Lawes, B.Sc., M.Ed., Ph.D.
Children at School
What has psychology to offer in educating our children? Can it help to formulate aims of education? What does it contribute to the understanding of learning and teaching?
How do differing views of childhood influence thinking about schooling? Are all children sufficiently the same to be treated the same? How can we "know" our pupils? What difference should we recognise?

Rev. Professor Leslie Francis, M.A., M.Sc., M.Th., B.D., Ph.D., F.B.Ps.S., F.C.P.
Clergy personality, stress and burnout
This workshop discusses the findings from a series of empirical studies among male and female clergy, exploring the relationship between individual differences in personality, ways of modelling ministry and levels of stress and burnout. Particular attention is drawn to the feminine characteristics of some male clergy and the masculine characteristics of some female clergy.

Dr. William K. Kay
Youth
The place of religion in adolescent development. Various theories of religious development, focusing on both Christianity and the educational implications of what is presently known.
This session will be based on work done at Carmarthen by Dr. Kay and Professor Leslie Francis.

Rev. Dr. Bruce Reed, M.A., M.Litt., Th.L.
The Psycho-dynamics of Life and Worship
To propose that human life is continually moving between predictable states of mind, and that such movement is a major condition for the well-being of society.
The lecture will trace out the dynamics of that process indicating how worship, work, symbolism, community, creativity, and vulnerability contribute to energise that process. The factors and powers which distort the process and render it dysfunctional will be considered.

Rev. Professor Leslie Francis, M.A., M.Sc., M.Th., Ph.D., F.B.Ps.S., F.C.P.
Jesus the Psychologist
This presentation employs the Myers-Briggs model of personality types to explore the gospel accounts of Jesus' understanding of individual difference among people. For example, in the parable of the Prodigal Son attention is drawn to the contrasting personalities of the older (I.S.F.J.) and the younger (E.N.T.P) brothers.

PART ONE
Lectures

INTRODUCTION TO THE THEME
Dr. K. B. Everard,

Those of us who knew Bill Gowland will carry with them memories of his distinctive attributes. For me these included an intuitive grasp of applied psychology. His ability to size people up, inspire them and motivate them was born of a deep love for his fellow human beings and a profound respect for their talents and strengths.

I fell under his spell in the late 1970s and have been associated with several of his initiatives ever since. he foresaw more clearly than most of us the impact of technology on work, the return of unemployment, and the growing synergy between science and religion.

It is fitting to his memory that the Ninth Consultation should be entirely devoted to the behavioural sciences - or the human or social sciences by which this field of endeavour is also known. They are regarded as the newest of the sciences, astronomy being the oldest, followed by physics, chemistry and biology, although the first psychometric test in recorded history is described in the Book of Judges (7.4-7), when Gideon selected 300 alert soldiers for his army to fight the Midianites,.

Although we often think of the Cosmos as that aspect of the Creation which is 'up there', Bill always reminded us that God's creative work continues 'down here'. St. Paul wrote: 'For through Him God created everything in heaven and on earth, the seen and the unseen things, including spiritual powers, lords, rulers and authorities' (Colossians 1:16). And again, 'Everyone must obey the state authorities, because no authority exists without God's permission and the existing authorities have been put there by god' (Romans 12:1). Clearly, then, the study of observed human behaviour, of the properties of the human mind, and of human institutions, which form the essence of psychology and sociology, are encompassed within the cosmos which Christ is redeeming.

In this introductory chapter I want to establish some links between the natural and behavioural sciences and between them and the Christian faith. However, I also want to offer an overview of this vast, fascinating field, largely from a laypersons's point of view, because I am not a *qualified* psychologist or sociologist: I spent half my ICI career as a polymer chemist and plastics technologist before moving on to applying behavioural science as an education and training manager and organisation development adviser. I believe I have seen the hand of God at work in this scene, and I hope that you too will discern it as you move through the chapters of this book.

At school I was captivated by physics and chemistry and obtained my degrees in the Natural Sciences at Oxford University. But I also read some of the works of Sigmund Freud in my mid-teens, and found these engrossing too. And I remember both reading and heeding an excellent book by C A Mace on *The Psychology of Study* to which it is fair to attribute some of my academic attainments.

I never had the chance to pursue my interest in psychology until I became personal assistant to Sir Alexander (later Lord) Fleck, the then Chairman of ICI. I shared an office with Tom Cottrell, also a chemist, and later to become the first Principal of Stirling University. We spent many hours discussing the psychology of learning, and we each had the opportunity to apply these ideas in later life.

Some time later, when I became responsible for developing PVC compounds for manufacturing rainwater goods, I met on a customer visit to Allied Ironfounders their technical manager, a man who later became the Reverend Dr. George Tolley, Canon of Sheffield Cathedral and Principal of Sheffield Polytechnic. The three of us had this in common: we were all able to see the synergy between the natural and the behavioural sciences, and between science and religion, and to do something about it.

Bill Gowland was a great admirer of space technology. I once gave him an example of this synergy, in relation to that momentous NASA enterprise, getting a man on the moon. The lunar module was built by a firm called TRW Systems. The success of the moonshot depended not only on getting all the complex technical systems to work; it also depended crucially on developing a social system which would enable

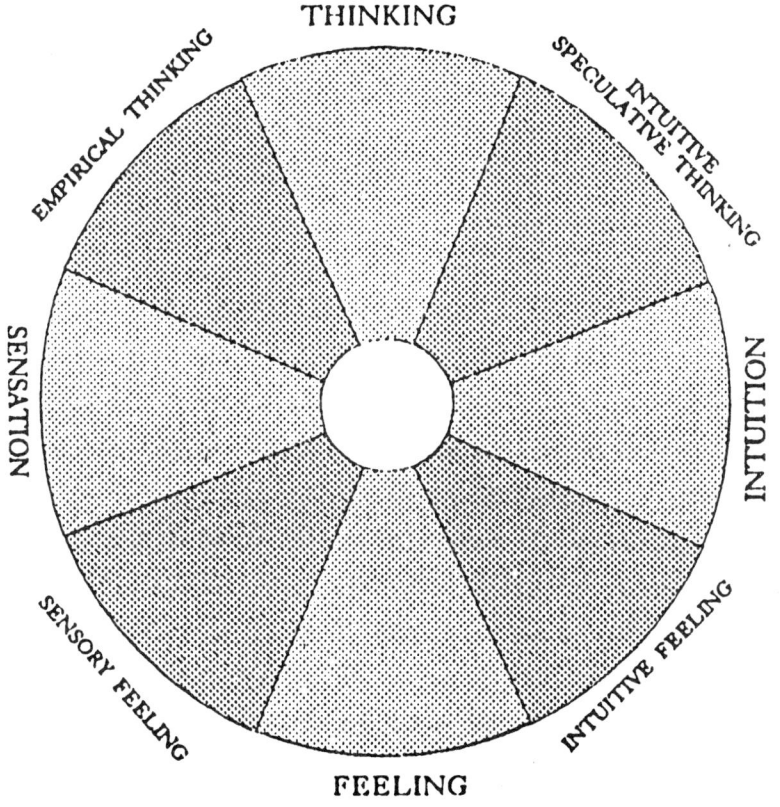

Dr Jolande Jacobi's Jungian Wheel - (1942).

Figure 1a

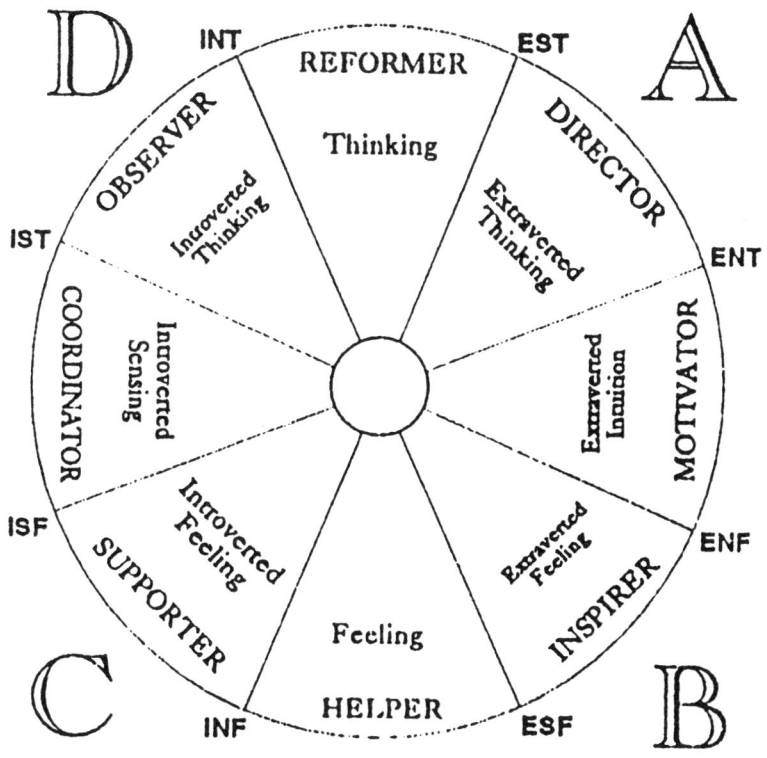

The 'Insights' Wheel - Carl Jung's psychological types in Dr Jolande Jacobi's setting.

Figure 1b

an army of technical specialists from different disciplines to collaborate in making them work. To this end TRW Systems employed a Harvard Professor Herb Shepherd, and a team of consultants, to employ the latest behavioural science technology alongside the engineering technology. It was one of the greatest triumphs of behavioural science this century, though some might claim the part it played in gaining *rapprochement* between the superpowers, or between the Arabs and Israelis in bringing peace to the Middle East.

I mention this particularly to physical scientists, who may be tempted to disparage the behavioural sciences as 'unscientific', as did the ICI physical chemist who said to me when I moved from technical work to behavioural science, 'Bertie, you are making a big mistake: you are prostituting science by pretending that it can be applied to behaviour'. But I am convinced that the selfsame scientific methods that I learned at this University as a physical chemist are equally applicable to the study of human and organisational behaviour. For example, Le Chatelier's and Heisenberg's principles, and Ashby's law of requisite variety, all have their counterparts in human systems. In Chemistry we arrange elements in the Periodic Table; in psychology we arrange individuals into psychological types, which we can characterise by measurement. Figure 1 identifies eight psychological types, based on Jung's theories. It is not difficult to guess that Bill Gowland was a mixture of ESF and ENF, whereas I am an INT (those familiar with Myers-Briggs can add a 'J'). Bill, of course, had a knack of motivating people even when they did not feel like being motivated.

LEARNING CYCLE AND LEARNING STYLES

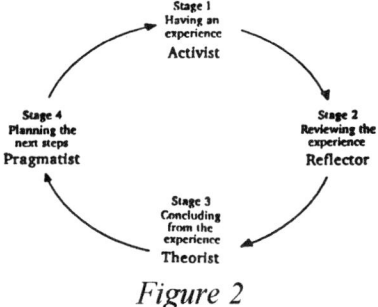

Figure 2

There are other ways of classifying individuals, e.g. preferred 'learning styles' (figure 2). When we were designing the Consultation, we debated whether we should make it more experiential than those that had gone before. Not everyone can maintain concentration on a lecture for an hour: they want to be up doing something. They are the 'Activists' and 'Pragmatists', while the 'Theorists' and 'Reflectors' prefer to sit and listen and think.

Any activists and pragmatists who quickly get satiated by listening to Consultation speakers may like to do something practical, using a paper from *The Social Psychology Newsletter*, no. 29(1993) on 'The Observational Study of Conference Participants'. It presents a typology of participants (presenters and audience alike) and offers clues that enable one to categorise one's friends and neighbours. For the rest of us, the more we are able to engage in all four learning styles, the more we are likely to take from any Consultation.

To return to the relationship between the physical and the behavioural sciences: I mentioned some similarities, and indeed I think there is a convergent trend between them. Traditionally, physical scientists have emphasised quantification and measurement, objectivity, the separation of the subject and the experimenter, and the creation of general laws. Mostly they work on problems that they believe they have a chance to solve. Behavioural scientists, by contrast, like engineers and doctors, work on problems that urgently need solving - where a person or a system is 'hurting'. You might therefore expect physical science to advance at the more rapid rate. Yet increasingly those who fund the physical scientists are expecting practical results: research that has no greater impact, in the words of my old physics teacher, the late Lord Bowden, than that of a feather dropping on the bottom of an empty well, is going out of fashion. So the prevailing scientific method is having to change to that most suited to solving the problem in hand.

Mapping the Behavioural Sciences: the 'Tree of Knowledge'
When natural scientists stray into the field of the behavioural sciences, they are apt to be bewildered by the complexity, because these sciences are like a tree with many branches and twigs, some of which

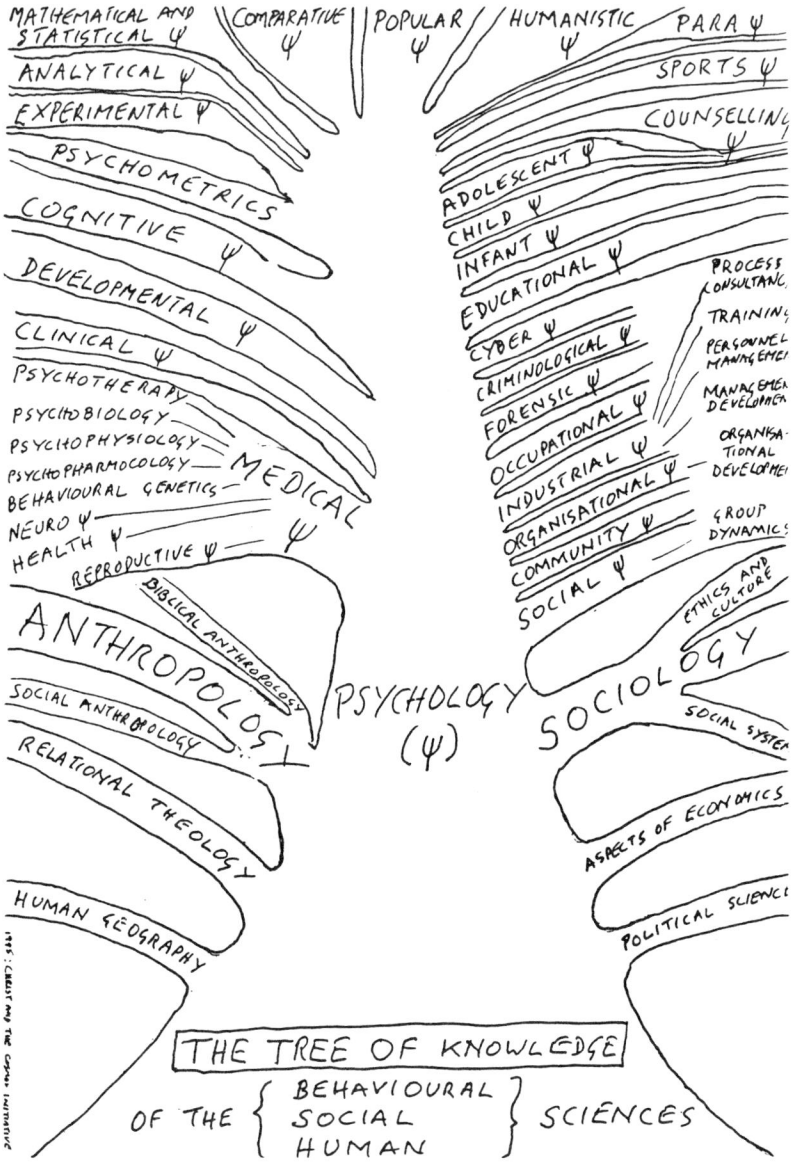

Figure 3

intertwine. I have therefore sketched this tree (figure 3), and I want to show how the behavioural sciences permeate so many aspects of our human experience.

First, the name of the tree: 'behavioural sciences' has a more modern tang than the term, 'social sciences' - like the Netherlands and Holland. The main trunk is psychology and the main branches are anthropology and sociology, but there are important links to other disciplines such as geography, economics and political science, and even to theology and religion. Indeed on the practical side, there is even a psychometric test that can place you on a spiritual relationship scale, which assesses the extent to which you perceive yourself as having a relationship with God.

Moving up the trunk, the most ramified science is psychology - so much so that I have to been able to fit in some of the blossoming twigs like psycholinguistics and psychoneuroimmunology. Nor have I included words like behaviourism, gestalt, developmentalism, structuralism, functionalism, habituation, sensitisation, conditioning, libido, depression, anxiety, obsession, repression, aptitude, attitude, inferiority complex and so on. However, these all form part of the canopy of the tree.

The biggest branches of psychology, in terms of the 1994 numbers of qualified practitioners, are: clinical (2810), counselling (1164), educational (1095) and occupational (745) psychology. In terms of membership of the British Psychological Society's research groups, the occupational psychology section is easily the largest at 2302, although many of these are not *qualified* practitioners.

If you include practitioners who have not got a degree or diploma in psychology, or even an A-level, then counselling is a huge area, in which 50,000 people are employed to deliver advice, guidance and counselling; at least 500,000 do so voluntarily and 2 million have a counselling unction in their job description. This includes churchpeople, but we ought to distinguish between those exercising lay pastoral care in fellowship and those trained in listening or counselling. Reputable bodies like the National Association of Counselling and Relate provide such training. Since there will never be enough fully qualified counsellors, psychologists, ministers, GPs or psychiatrists to cope with other than the more extreme human problems, and to train others to do so, the rest play a vital supportive role in society.

Those involved in applying psychology are called by other names than 'applied psychologists'. Since 1966 I have lived in amongst the branches on the extreme right of the figure. One gets 'qualified' by experience and being taught on short courses.

Soon there will probably be occupational standards of competence in applied psychology for such people, on which it is hoped will be based National and Scottish Vocational Qualifications (NVQs and SVQs). The great value of NVQs is that they promote lateral transfer of knowledge and sill between fragmented disciplines, and I welcome them.

Some academic psychologists get uncomfortable when 'amateurs' like myself encroach on their territory. No doubt some people make false intellectual claims in the name of science, and criticism is then appropriate, as in any science; it should be based on empirical evidence. Even qualified psychologists are open to such criticism (an indeed disciplinary action) if they stray beyond their field of competence. However, I believe there are instances when exclusion of 'amateurs' by professional gate-keepers goes too far, e.g. in the application of psychometric tests.

Nevertheless, the BPS does not recognise the need to 'give away' psychology to non-psychologists in other professions. It contributes to popularisation of the genuine discipline by publishing self-help books. What it disapproves of is the publication of unscientific literature about bogus psychology - the equivalent of astrology in relation to astronomy. Unfortunately the boundary between the bogus and the scientific is not always clear. Eysencks's 'Test Your IQ', Edward do Bono's books and some newspaper quizzes are regarded as being somewhere near the watershed, for example, however useful they have proved to be for some readers.

Bill Gowland, of course, believed that professional scientists, for whom he had a great respect, have a duty to share the wonder and the awe of their field of study with the person in the pew, because it is all part of the Creation, and an exciting part at that. This book attempts to fulfil that mission. But the process of diffusion of psychology to the general public has been largely unexplored by academics.

There is no doubt about the latent interest: don't most of us read the psychological features in our newspapers, do the personality tests (even though some may compare them to horoscopes), browse in the psychology section of libraries and bookshops, and maybe buy books on intimate relationships? We lay participants at the Consultation owe a debt of gratitude to the eminent psychologists who shared their insights with us, and then wrote these chapters. Several whom we approached refused the invitation.

And whereabout is God in this tree? Well, of course, He is all over, and different people will find Him in different places. Words more familiar to theologians like healing, nurture, wholeness, soul, ministry, reconciliation, Kingdom and redemption can be overlaid on the diagram; they form part of the canopy of the tree.

However, not every scientist believes this. Francis Crick, for example, who discovered DNA, calls each one of us 'no more than the behaviour of a vast assembly of nerve cells....' *(The Astonishing Hypothesis. The Scientific Search for the Soul)*. He seems blind to the social aspects of human nature, which have a bearing on the metaphysical. It is the interaction of the neuronal systems with physical systems in the environment, and through these to other neuronal systems, that is important.

Some scientists argue that it is only a matter of time before artificial intelligence will be able to simulate all aspects of the human mind. This is where the mechanistic or reductionist approach to science, and the drive for ever more simple but powerful theories, leads to. There is, however, no scientific evidence that the human mind will ever be fully explicable in terms of the electrochemistry of the brain. Properties like personality and the soul must be discussed in another language, although there may be parallels between the concept of 'fields' in physics and 'Spirit' in theology. A study of human nature in the round must seek to integrate the physico-chemical, the psychological, the sociological, the cultural and the theological perspectives if we are to recognise that human beings are both natural and spiritual creatures, just as electrons and light are both waves and particles.

Indeed, the psychologist, Robert Barry, in a book entitled *A Theory of Almost Everything*, argues that a new psychology is beginning to emerge that will stretch the discipline beyond its present limits. It will be both transpersonal and holistic - transpersonal in that it takes us beyond the narrow self and holistic in that it embraces the entire cosmos in the recognition that everything is connected to everything else - 'members one of another'. The philosopher Birch talks of our metaphysical chaos - a sense of separation from the 'whole scheme of things', because we have no conviction that there is any scheme of things or values in the universe. 'If we have no value for the cosmos', he asks, 'can there be any value or meaning within human life, in human relationships and in our relationship to the environment?'

A Growing Branch

By way of emplifying the connectedness of physical and psychological research, I will now describe some work going on in the neruopsychological field.

Unless there are beings on other planets, the most complex and fully developed structure in the whole cosmos is probably the human brain. Your and my brain each contain about 10 billion cells, or 'neurons', which is approximately equal to the number of trees in the Amazon rain-forest. Each cell has between 1000 and 10,000 connections with other cells, so the total number is roughly equal to the number of leaves in the forest. The brain works electrochemically. It is what organises human behaviour and, through it, organisational behaviour. It can understand and model the cosmos. It is the organ that enables us to relate to God and He to us. Could there be a more fascinating subject of scientific study than the brain, and the mind it organises? When we have a theory of everything, and understand our own minds, shall we discover the mind of God, as Stephen Hawking put it?

Psychology is about how the mind works. It is also the study of the soul. It is a complementary study to the electrochemistry of the brain.

Two years ago I volunteered to take part in some experimental research funded by the Medical Research Council at Hammersmith Hospital. They wanted someone with a normal brain! I found when I got there that they were going to inject into my blood-stream 5 millisieverts of radioactive water, irradiated in a cyclotron. Fortunately, having attended previous Christ and the Cosmos Consultations, I was able to recognise that this is no more than equivalent to two years' natural radiation; it is the maximum permitted for Sellafield workers. So my life expectancy is not shortened by much.

Because the brain at work consumes a lot of oxygen, the radioactive isotope ^{15}O migrates preferentially to areas of high brain activity. There it disintegrates, emitting positrons. These travel only about 1-2 mm before they collide with negative electrons, thus annihilating one another and emitting high-energy gamma-rays in opposite directions. These shot out of my head and were detected as pairs by specialised detectors, which fed the signals into a computer.

At the same time I was operating a joy-stick, connected to a humble BBC computer, in one of four directions, in response to regular bleeps. In the second experiment, I was told just to imagine that I was moving the joy-stick, without actually moving it. the experimenters could, in effect, read my thoughts, because both the imagination of these movements and their implementation were separately recorded on the PET scanner (PET = Positron Emission Tomography). Figure 4 is a picture, rather like those radar maps of rain activity on our weather forecasts, of my brain at work (the original photograph was coloured)

There were five other experimental subjects and figure 5 shows you what our brains look like with a nuclear magnetic resonance imaging scanner, which they also used in the experiment (taken from Stephan et al. 'Functional Anatomy of the Mental Representation of Upper

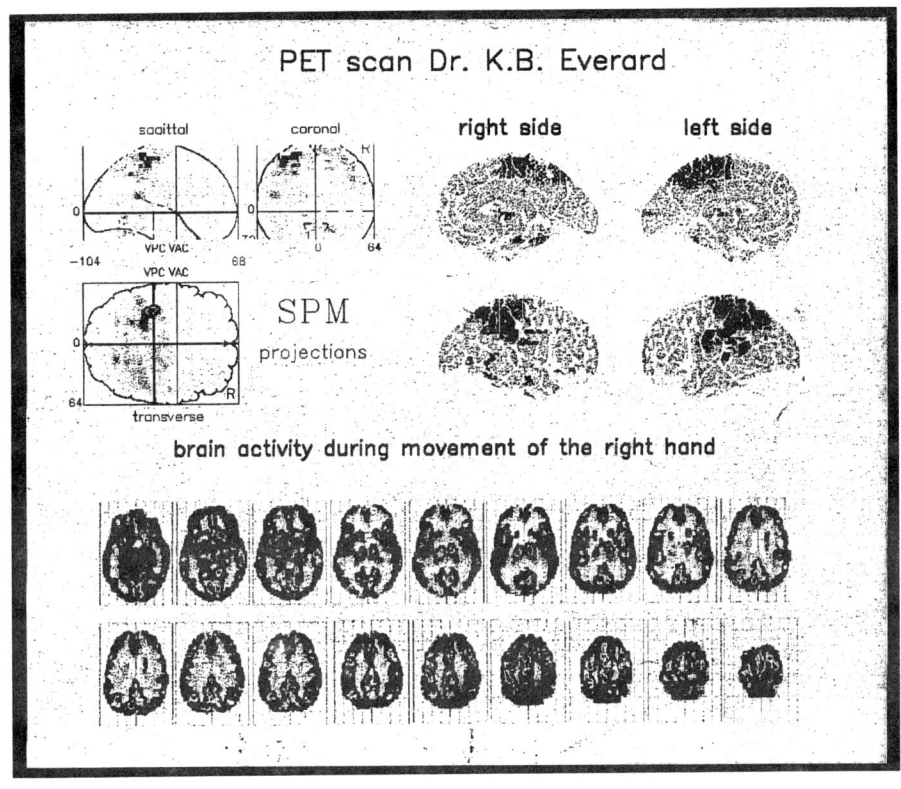

Figure 4

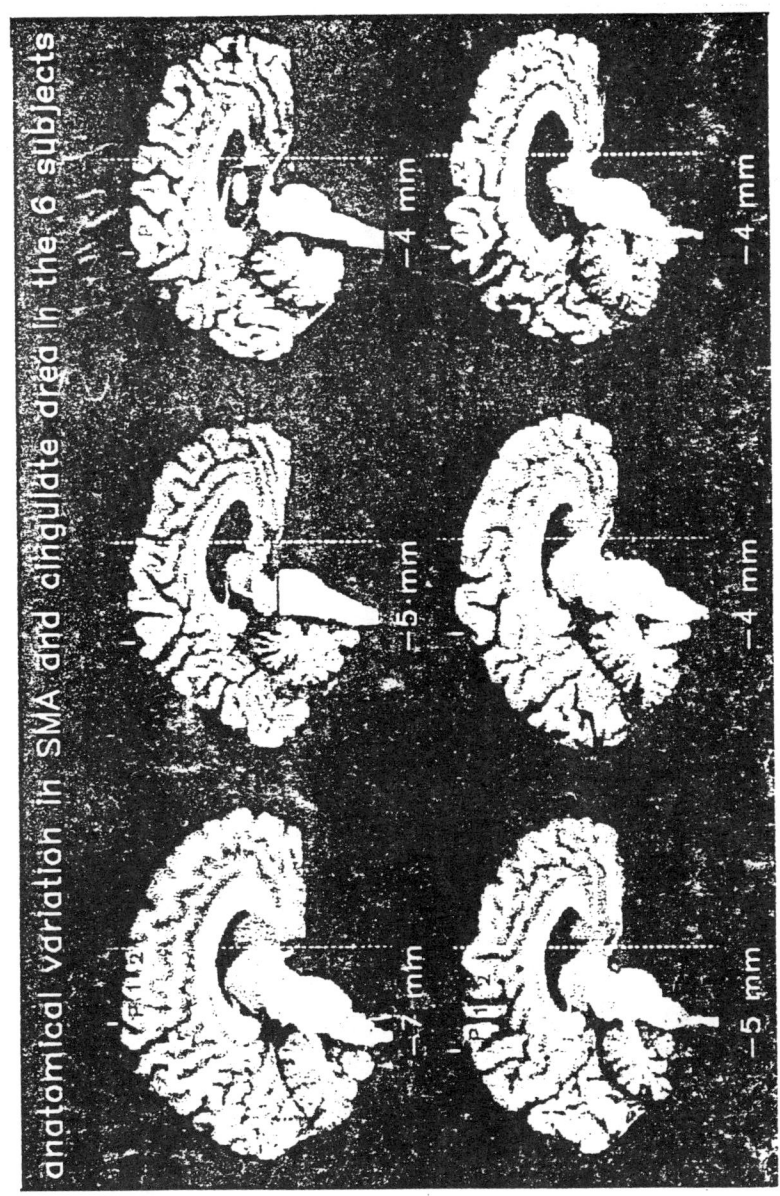

Figure 5

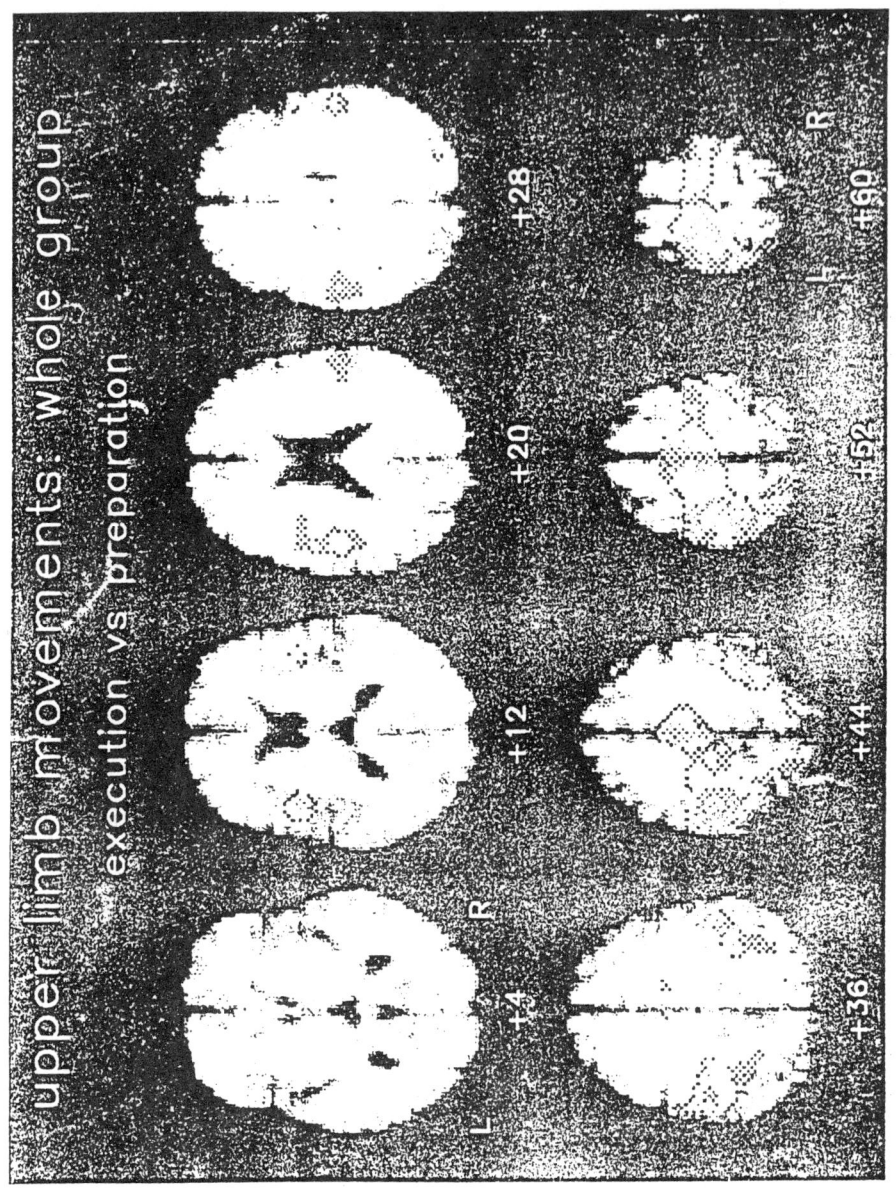

Figure 6

Extremity Movements in Healthy Subjects', *Journal of Neurophysiology*, 1995, 73, 373). No prizes are given for guessing which is my brain: I'll give you a clue - men's brains are bigger than woman's!

Figure 6 are PET scans of brain sections showing where the brain is most active in imagining, preparing for and executing the joy-stick movements. Imagining and executing these movements engage different parts of the brain. Interestingly, the precise site of the activity varied with the individual anatomy of us subjects.

The practical object of this research was to assist in improving the rehabilitation of stroke victims. Treatment differs according to whether they have lost their power to imagine movements or to implement them. However, the same techniques are also used to identify where brain activity takes place when subjects are hearing words, seeing words, speaking words and generating words. And Susan Greenfield's Royal Institution Christmas lectures, broadcast on BBC TV in January 1995, showed PET scans of depressive activity, thus linking brain metabolism to psychological states.

PET scans have shown that men and women display different kinds of brain activity when they are experiencing emotions such as pleasure, fear and happiness. There are distinct gender differences, according to Ruben Gur, Professor of Neuropsychology at the University of Pennsylvania. On the evolutionary time-scale, parts of the human brain are shared with those of moneys and reptiles. Women are like monkeys in using a more developed part of the brain for their emotions, whereas men are like reptiles.

Yet another line of research is leading towards the implantation of electronic chips in the head, in order to link brain activity directly to external computers. This could restore feeling and movement to paralysed limbs, and even perhaps create human emotion and sensations such as touch and smell. In theory it is possible to do away with keyboards; you just imagine the movement you want to make by thinking of the letter you want to type, and the required signal could be relayed direct to your computer. However, all that is a long way away, and not all of us may want to have our innermost thoughts opened up to the Internet! Injecting radioactive water into the blood-stream or implanting chips in the head are unacceptably intrusive techniques for finding out what is going on in the brain. Happily, however, there are less intrusive techniques, one of which is being increasingly used in management training and other fields. This rejoices in the unfortunate name of 'neurolinguistic programming' (NLP), on which several books have now been written for managers, trainers and communicators in general. This branch of psychology originated in the mid-1970s when a linguist and a computer scientist started to model excellent communication in the field of psychotherapy. They explored what was happening when two people miscommunicated; for example, if I utter the word 'training', some of you will interpret it as the sort of thing you do to dogs. It has overtones that get in the way of *my* meaning, which is more to do with human growth and development. Even the phrase 'Christ and the Cosmos' introduces problems of communication: I am sure we lost an excellent speaker because he put a different interpretation on the phrase from that which Bill meant when he coined it. Indeed, one clergyman told me that until we changed the title of these consultations, we would not get all the people we wanted to come to them.

NLP is a branch of psychology which has progressed by observing a person's eye movements as they are talking, and relating these movements to the metaphoric language in which they are speaking. Communication of one to another depends on our ability to access our thoughts, translate them into spoken words, which we then convey to others via sound waves. The receiver then has to detect the sound-waves, translate them back into words, and then feed them into the brain so as to generate mental images or thoughts which resemble those in the brain of the transmitter.

It turns out that there are three main ways of thinking:
- images (visual)
- sound/words (auditory)
- feelings (kinesthetic)

Visualisation

Visual constructed images

Visual remembered images

Constructed sounds

Remembered sounds

*Kinesthetic
(Feelings and bodily
sensations)*

*Auditory Digital
(Internal dialogue)*

Figure 7

Our eye movements reflect the mode of thinking we are adopting, as figure 7 shows. Our patterns of language and modes of expression follow our thoughts. However, the receiver's mental images may not correspond with ours, unless he or she detects and interprets the eye movements of the speaker.

This linguistic process is quite complicated, and by understanding it, it is possible to improve person-to-person communication. We can train people to become better communicators and more powerful influencers, especially in that difficult area of changing values and beliefs.

Painstaking observation, in this case of eye movements, is not, of course, the only way in which influencers have been helped to become more effective. The very first course I attended on being appointed an education and training manager in 1966 was on skills of persuasion. It was an ICI course, mainly for sales representatives, which has run for at least three decades. It is based on the meticulous observation, in a project conducted by the American Sales Analysis Institute, of what precisely distinguished effective salesmen from the average. Things like body language, use of questions, the pace of communication and the sequence of presentation of ideas were all recorded and analysed for their effect on buyer behaviour. The training that was base don this analysis sometimes had unexpected effects: the wife of one of our sales representatives, a few weeks after he had attended the course, exclaimed 'Darling, I just don't understand what's come over you: you have been so nice to me since you went away on that course!'

So I believe we can turn psychological understanding to desirable ends. We can *learn* to display the Christian virtues of love and empathy. We can learn to be become fishers of men and women. And the churches are missing out unless they get abreast of these approaches. Didn't Bill once say 'Why should the Devil have all the fun?' Equally these techniques can be misapplied in the wrong hands, as the more outlandish religious cults have shown.

Another example of valuable training I received was entitled 'The Practice of Teamwork'. The late Ralph Coverdale designed it. He was a Jesuit psychologist who worked closely with Bernard Babington-Smith, a psychology lecturer in Oxford University. It showed a group how to become members one of another. It was deeply rooted in observational techniques. The themes were the practical outworkings of Christian values. Those courses prospered: ICI put thousands through them. Worldwide, over a quarter of a million people have learned to practise teamwork iwth the Coverdale organisation. Over 30 local education authorities engaged Coverdale as consultants. The Oxford LEA has tried it successfully with school children at Yarnton Primary School. The children think it great! Teambuilding is the most frequently used method of developing managers and organisations; in a recent survey it not only came top of about 90 different approaches; the 600 respondents expected it to remain top in the foreseeable future. It is having a profound effect on the way organisations are run. It is one of the great triumphs of applied psychology, in which I detect the hand of God at work.

The Development of Psychology

I have only given a few examples of contemporary development in the behavioural sciences. Let me finally try to trace the development of the discipline and look into its future.

The science of self became established towards the end of the 19th century. William James published his *Principles of Psychology* in 1890, and Sigmund Freud *The Interpretation of Dreams* in 1900. Freud postulated the division of the mind into the conscious, thinking *ego*, the childishly impulsive *id* and the *superego* which acts as conscience and upholder of standards. This is not far from St. Paul's analysis: 'For what our human nature wants [the *id*] is opposed to what the Spirit wants [the *superego*], and what the Spirit wants is opposed to what our human nature wants' (Galations 5:17). And again, 'Each one should judge his own conduct' (6:4); in other words we need to become conscious of our own behaviour [the *ego*].

Although James rode on the central tide of psychology, Freud was more of an extremist, but he certainly created a wave. A second wave of development occurred in the early twentieth century when the behaviourists lined up the science of self with other sciences such as physics. This rested not on a hypothesis about the make-up of the mind, but on observation and measurement of behaviour. It excluded the subjective data of consciousness, and phenomena such as love, art and religion. Nevertheless it was a fruitful period. Meanwhile the tide of empirical research flowed on.

A third wave of development came in the second half of this century in the form of humanistic psychology. It was a reaction against the excessively mechanistic and deterministic views of humanity espoused by the behaviourists and the psychoanalysts. it led to the human potential movement, one of whose proponents was Abraham Maslow. He propounded a 'hierarchy of human needs' (figure 8),

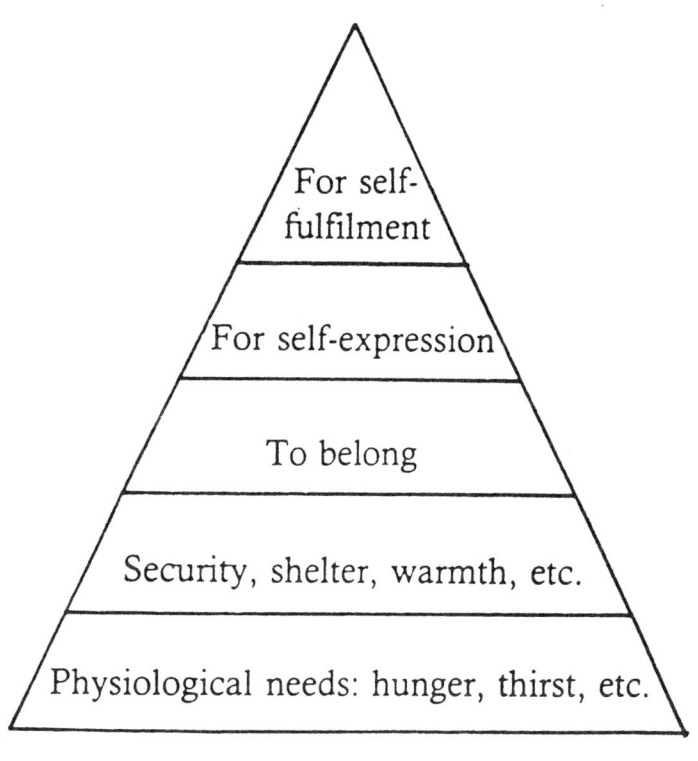

Figure 8

whose apex was self-actualisation or self-fulfilment. He is sometimes accused of deifying the self, but in his later writings he recognised the existence of something over and above and beyond the self, in other words self-transcendence - a capacity for mystical and spiritual experiences in altered states of consciousness. This enables connections to be made with various Eastern philosophies as well as with Christianity.

Humanistic psychology has many practical applications. With it, Carl Rogers transformed the practice of counselling. Dick Beckhard and others opened up the whole new field of organisation development, which was widely applied in ICI while he was the behavioural science consultant to the Board for over 25 years. Professor Andrew Pettigrew's book, *The Awakening Giant*, is the story of this development. Sir John Harvey-Jones played a leading part, and one chapter describes the work that I led.

Personal growth, 'learning for life', the 'learning organisation' and community development are all outcrops of humanistic psychology. It shares with the Christian religion a vision of hope: the notion that individuals and society have only to shake off their chains to realise their tremendous potential for development. As the physical universe is expanding, so is the mind. There is ever more to encompass and understand, much more to perceive, much more to do. We grow more broad-minded as knowledge expands.

Humanistic psychology is not without its dangers: it has been blamed for bringing about the selfish society - 'doing one's own thing'. But this is not a necessary outcome of its application. It is a consequence of leaving out God. Over 50 years ago, Carl Jung saw this danger: her pointed out that if we lose our spiritual values we shall pay the price in terms of social disintegration and moral decay.

What we need to do now is to explore the extension of self, to go beyond self-consciousness into an awareness of being something that is much greater than self - a 'cosmic consciousness'. The theme is one of interconnectedness, between body, mind and spirit, and between individual, social system and environment: members one of another, embracing all.

Alvin Toffler in his book *The Third Wave* concludes that a new civilisation is forming, and that we are experiencing the break-up of the industrial revolution, just as it displaced the agricultural revolution. He says that we are the children of the next transformation. We face a quantum leap forwards - an enlargement of the human consciousness.

The scientist, Paul Davies, sees a wholly rational explanation of the world as impossible; we have to progress to a different concept of 'understanding' from that of rational explanation. It is here that science and theology meet. One the one hand we have the continuous expansion and understanding of consciousness (the 'push' factor, as Robert Barry calls it); on the other is progressive divine revelation (the 'pull' factor).

As we contemplate the future unfolding of these developments, let the last words be St. Paul's:

> I consider that what we suffer at this present time cannot be compared at all with the glory that is going to be revealed to us. All of creation waits with eager longing for God to reveal His sons. For creation was condemned to lose its purpose, not of its own will, but because God willed it to be so. Yet there was the hope that creation itself would one day be set free from its slavery to decay and would share the glorious freedom of the children of God. For we know that up to the present time all of creation groans with pain, like the pain of childbirth. But it is not just creation alone that groans; God's gifts also groan within ourselves, as we wait for God to make us His sons and set our whole being free.
>
> Romans 8:18-23

I owe a debt of gratitude to David Booth, a fellow chemist now Professor of Psychology at the University of Birmingham, for his painstaking critique of a draft of this chapter and for his invaluable suggestions for its improvement.

Psychology and Religion
Dr. Michael Argyle

The problems raised by science for religion have come mainly from the physical sciences and more recently the biological ones. Psychology leads to quite different issues. It might be thought that both psychology and religion have similar aims - to understand human life and help us to live it better, and as a result they would have a lot in common. In fact they are totally different, and theologians and religious folk know as little about psychology as most psychologists know about religion, i.e. nothing, or possibly less since what they think they know is usually wrong. I should make clear that by religion here I shall be thinking primarily of the Christian religion, and by psychology I shall mean the corpus of scientific knowledge which is being gathered in University departments and research institutes throughout the world; I shall not mean psychoanalysis, or other clinical or philosophical approaches not based on experimental or statistical research.

Since their approaches are so different it is not surprising that there are several points of tension, or even confrontation; I shall discuss three of them in this chapter. (1) Psychology seeks to explain human behaviour, and has had some success in doing so, without reference to religion, (2) it also seeks to explain religious behaviour and experience in the same way, and (3) it tries to tackle human problems, such as mental health, in a different way from religion, and has some success in doing this. In psychology as in physics a considerable sense of mystery remains, such as how consciousness arises from physiology, and in what sense we have free will.

However science is not our only source of knowledge. Mathematics, morals, our knowledge of the social word and other people, and religion, we acquire in other ways. All are based on through or experience without resort to scientific data, and our conscious, subjective experience is quite different from science. Psychology can study why people believe things or engage in religious behaviour, and what effect it has on them, but these are different issues from whether or not it is true. The physics of music, which is now studied on some music courses: it can show how sounds are produced, and how to do so better, but tells us very little about music. Study of the horticulture of rose growing can tell us how to do it, but nothing about the beauty of the rose. In each of these cases science has shown how to do something, but has been irrelevant to the inner experience involved, and cannot say whether the experience is valid. I don't think therefore that psychology can either prove or disprove religious beliefs, but it may be able to tell us something about religion. It is also possible that it might tell us something positive from the study of religious, moral and other experience; our knowledge of religion is based on these experiences; psychology studies such experiences systematically.

Many early psychologists were "behaviourists", that is they mainly studied animals, and ignored or discounted conscious experience; reports of it were sometimes included as "verbal behaviour". There are no behaviourists now, they are extinct. This is because there has been a "cognitive revolution" in psychology, which recognises not only conscious experience, but many contents of the mind. These include ways of categorising events, words for these categories, rules, plans, values, theories and explanations, and whole worlds of experience, including mathematics, morals, the arts, and religion. In the case of mathematics, the principles seem to be there to be discovered, they are not invented, they have a kind of Platonic sphere of existence. Assessment of the truth of mathematical theorems is not done by machine, but by human judgements (Penrose 1989). Those who use logarithms may not fully understand them, but can use them and find that they work. The elements in these subjective worlds operate in a similar way, in that they have complex meanings through their relations with other terms, as with cricket, the law, and the Trinity. The elements may also have emotional associations, they may be associated with joy, fear, or ecstasy. They are not part of the physical world, they are part of the inner, cognitive world. They have been brought into psychology because they are needed to explain behaviour. Ideas, like values, beliefs and rules, can override the effects of biological drives. For example a person who is hungry may not eat, because he or she is fasting, slimming, or on an Oxfam demonstration. Language is an important part of the inner world. If your vocabulary includes the terms orange (i.e. the colour), honour, chutzpah, forgiveness, for example, this will affect behaviour. Rules are important; if you want to play cricket you must master a whole set of rules, and these are framed in terms of a whole set of concepts such as "not out", "lbw", etc.

Consciousness has been as the greatest unsolved scientific problem, the "ultimate mystery". Psychologists, philosophers, neurologists and workers in machine intelligence have put a lot of work in here (Marcel and Bisiach, 1988). It is generally agreed that consciousness is the result of evolution, and that it must therefore give some biological advantage. This could be (1)the capacity to solve new problems, deal with new situations, (2)being able to imagine the consequences of different possible acts, or (3)a superior capacity to deal with other people, through being able to imagine their point of view.

It is generally assumed that higher levels of neural process have merged, which have a subjective side, though it is not understood how these neural events become conscious, that we are conscious of sensory inputs, memories and images, and plans for future behaviour. The neural events which have a conscious side have a causal role in directing behaviour. This behaviour is intentional, based on reasons, takes account of values and long term plans, and the meaning of stimuli received. We are aware of the self, and it is the self which has plans. Patterns of causation can occur at the higher level of analysis; at the higher levels associated with consciousness there is volition, the choice, initiation and monitoring of behaviour, carried out by lower levels in the system. However we have no idea how consciousness is produced by these neural processes (Gray, 1987). Computer programmes can mimic some of these processes; for example chess-playing machines can "try out in imagination" a lot of alternative moves. This does not mean that chess-playing machines are conscious or are "thinking"; Searle (1984) argued that a person locked in a "Chinese room", equipped only with a rule book, could give the impression of speaking Chinese, though he had no knowledge of the language or the messages being received and answered. Machines have no sense of "meaning", and can't "understand" anything. There are some other differences between brains and computers: computers can only use the programmes which have been put in, they can't solve new problems, they stay the same and do not learn by experience, and they have far fewer elements and connections between them than brains have (Penrose, 1989). Machine intelligence experts are no longer prepared to say that machines which can play chess or mimic other kinds of thinking are "conscious" (D.Michie, personal communication).

A widely expressed view of human nature is that it is the result of evolution, in which we have gone further than the animals by acquiring language as well as consciousness; this has given us the power to make plan and decisions about our behaviour, which are based on rational considerations, and that this enables us to escape from having our behaviour determined by the biological urges of hunger, sex and the rest (Csikszentmihalyi, 1988). We also have the capacity to create new things, new sentences, new solutions to problems. Over the course of history new ideas which work or are popular are retained and built-up; this can be described as "social evolution" since no biological changes are involved, the new elements are passed on through education and socialisation. Moral and religious ideas have much of their origins in this way.

Many of these cognitions are socially shared, as in the case of language; they get into our heads as a result of social processes like education and parental socialisation. We learn our language, and other languages, and this has some parallel with putting WordPerfect into a computer. Socially shared materials may be experienced as a kind of "social reality", because everyone else has the same ideas. Each sphere has its own special means of validation; mathematics is by rational deduction, vocabulary by reference to dictionaries and past practice, history by reference to memories and records, rules and morals by consulting social authorities and moral leaders. For religion we turn to scripture, the church, and personal religious experience.

Beliefs

Religious people have a lot of "beliefs", but what exactly are beliefs? They are not like believing that Everest is in Tibet, or that it is time for tea. They are about highly abstract and mysterious entities, and questions about beliefs invite answers like "It depends what you mean by God". It is not known how many philosophers hold such beliefs since they say they can't understand the questions. Research on the percentage of individuals who believe in God find that this varies with how the question is put, and that more will say yes if there is an alternative for "some sort of spirit or vital force which controls life", as well as "a kind of person who watches over each of us" (Argyle and Beit-Hallahmi, 1975). Religious beliefs are part of a whole framework of ideas and words, and it is necessary to grasp these first. One of the main ways in which people come to hold beliefs is through being a member of a group which uses these words and ideas. It is less a matter of rational argument than of deciding to adopt a framework of ideas. This is what the "leap of faith" consists of; there really is such a leap in cases of sudden conversion, but for most individuals there is no leap but gradual socialisation.
In the case of "sudden" conversion it is clear that more than just cognitions is involved. These individuals have previously been in a state of distress and self-dissatisfaction, sometimes sexual guilt, the conversion is a kind of problem-solving, which is found to make sense and solve serious personal problems (Batson et al, 1993). They are tested by whether they work, sometimes by religious experiences, and by appeal to scripture and religious authorities. Every sphere of cognitions has its own means of verification.
A parallel to religious belief is undertaking a course of psychoanalysis. You have to adopt the ideas and the terminology. The parallel goes further than this; in psychoanalysis you adopt a whole style of thinking, daily or weekly rituals, and hope to be cured. To be cured you have to believe in the Ego, the Superego and the Id,

while to be saved you have to believe in the Father, Son and the Holy Ghost (R.H. Thouless, personal communication). Another parallel is deciding to get married. Here the leap of faith consists of adopting a new and shared way of life, in the hope that it will work; this too may be done by degrees. For it to work there has to be continued effort, as in psychoanalysis, and as in the case of religion.

These systems of ideas, which I called "collective representations", are sometimes called "social constructions" by sociologists (Berger and Luckman, 1967). This could be misleading, suggesting that the ideas are just human inventions, whereas they may be ways of thinking about an underlying reality. In mathematics logarithms can be seen as constructions, but they have their own validity and are found to work in the world. In California the state park now known as Yosemite was once just a piece of the wilderness, until it was socially constructed, with names for everything, facilities, rituals and a romantic history. But underneath all this human invention there is still a spectacular valley with magnificent waterfalls.

There are different ways of believing. Some believe that what it says in the Bible is literally true; this is the position of literalists and fundamentalists - and for all children under the age of 12. For those who find this position impossible there is the realisation that the words may stand for realities for which there is not language, though they may be expressed in ritual or music. The words may be understood as metaphors. This is very helpful, since it helps us understand abstract ideas in terms of more familiar concepts. So motivation in psychology may be understood as a kind of hydraulic system, or the Holy Spirit as a kind of "thin loving fog". However these beliefs are more than metaphors, if it is believed that they are really true. The same is true of poetry, which may add to our insights and understanding, with more than metaphors, since it points to an underlying reality.

Can psychology explain religious beliefs? Attempts to find reductionist explanations have on the whole failed. One of the more successful is interpreting belief in the after-life in terms of avoiding anxiety about impending death. It is found that the very old, and the terminally ill believe in it more than others (100% of those over 90 are usually found to hold this belief), and as we saw above this belief is successful in reducing anxiety. On the other hand the beliefs in judgement, hell, and the Devil are less easy to account for, since they would increase anxiety. Further hypotheses would be needed, such as the belief in a just world requiring some compensation in the next world, or hell-fire evangelism producing long-lasting beliefs. Other reductionistic theories have been less successful: there is very little evidence that God is a projected father figure, or that religion is due to deprivation (middle class people go to church twice as much as others), or is the result of having a particular kind of personality. And as I said above this strictly irrelevant to the truth or otherwise of beliefs. Many psychologists of religion do not take a reductionist approach, but rather accept the existence of religion as part of the social world in which people are reared, and that for them transcendence is part of their experience (Brown, 1987).

Does religion enhance well-being?

I turn now to some concrete empirical issues, where psychology can tell us something interesting about religion. It may also enable us to "evaluate" different kinds of religion, in terms of their earthly consequences. I will start with the well-being of believers, and then look at the consequences for prosocial behaviour.

Well-being (1) Happiness

Moberg and Taves (1965) used a measure of "adjustment" which was really self-reported happiness, in a study of 1,343 elderly people in Minnesota, and found that scores were much higher for those who were most active in the church, especially if they were single, old, retired or in poor health (Table 1)

TABLE 1 - Scores on an index of happiness, and church membership

	Church leaders	Other church members	Non-church members
Married	15	15	12
Widowed	15	11	7
Single	12	8	5
65-70	18	14	10
71-79	15	12	7

80 -	13	8	6
Fully employed	18	18	17
Partly employed	16	16	13
Fully retired	15	12	7
Health (self-rated)			
Excellent	17	14	13
Good	15	14	11
Fair	17	6	8
More active in religious organisations than in fifties	16	13	9
Less active	14	11	7

Source: Moberg and Taves (1965)

This is supported by supported by studies of social support and friendship in the church community. A number of studies have found that often people's closest friends share their religious beliefs. I have recently found that church members report a very high level of social support, and that 37% say that their church friends are closer than other friends; this is more than for any other "leisure" group (Table 2)

How close are your main relationships with other members of your group?

closer than other friendships		
	religious	37%
	voluntary work	29%
	total	11%
very similar		
	musical	78%
	social	54%
	sport	41%
	dancing	40%
	total	40%
different		
	political	60%
	voluntary work	43%
	evening classes	43%
	total	22%
less close		
	sport	40%
	evening classes	37%
	hobbies	33%
	total	27%

The explanation of this result is not yet known. It could be due to the high level of self disclosure, particularly at house groups, to the sharing of deeply held beliefs and values, or possibly to feelings of contrast and separation from the out group.
However in other studies, church attendance has been held constant statistically, and two other sources of well-being due to religion have been found. Feeling close to God, as a result of prayer, religious experiences, and other private devotions is one factor (Pollner, 1989). The other is certainty of beliefs, especially for old people; Southern Baptists in the USA are happy for this reason.
Perhaps "happiness" is not the most appropriate measure for studying the benefits of religion. Indeed it has been found that the aspect of happiness most affected by religion is a sense of meaning and purpose (Chamberlain and Zika, 1988).
(detailed references to this and the later sections will be found in Beit-Hallahmi, Brown and Argyle, in press).

(2) Mental Health

There is a massive quantity of research on this topic. Batson et al (1993) re-analysed 115 such studies, and found that in most of them there was a statistical relationship between "intrinsic religiosity" and good mental health, and the opposite relationship with "extrinsic". By intrinsic religious it is meant taking religion as an end in itself, faith as "a supreme value in its own right", whereas extrinsic religiosity is using religion as a means to other ends. Religion has also been found to act as a "buffer" for stressful events, that is it prevents them from causing distress. This is partly done by various forms of "religious coping", such as taking God as a partner in taking decisions (Pargament et al 1988).
We have seen that religion is on the whole good for mental health, but this is not always so. A proportion of mental patients have religious ideas or preoccupations, such as believing themselves to be important religious figures. This is more common among working class fundamentalists. During the Millerite revival in 1842-3 in New England, nearly a quarter of mental hospital admissions were

diagnosed as "religious excitement", and there are later and present day reports that high pressure evangelism has had this kind of effect. Sects and cults were believed to have a bad effect at one time. However some cults have come out better than expected from a psychological point of view. Joining one is often good for mental health, despite the cognitive bondage, partly because the members have often been in a very poor condition to begin with, often on drugs, and have benefited from the intense social support and strong discipline. The worst casualties have been among those who have been forcibly removed and "deprogrammed" (Lewis and Bromley, 1987).

Serious, psychotic, disorders raise different issues. A proportion of mental patients are in a sense religious, such as the 50 a year with the "Jerusalem syndrome". Many religious leaders have been found to possess serious mental symptoms; however they are different from regular patients - they are well able to cope some of the time, and their ideas have a more universal appeal.

(3) Health

A celebrated study by Comstock and Partridge (1972) found that regular church goers in Maryland had much lower rates of death from a number of causes (Table 3).

Table 3 - Mortality rates of regular church-goers and others (per 1,000 over 5 years in most cases)

		Once a week or more	Less than once a week
Heart disease		38	89
Emphysema (3 years)	18	52	
Cirrhosis (3 years)	5	25	
Cancer of the rectum	13	17	
Suicide (6 years)	11	29	

However it has been objected that people who are too ill will not be able to get to church so the effect may be spurious. To get round this problem Dwyer et al (1990) studied church membership rates in

3,063 American counties and found that this correlated with lower rates of respiratory and digestive cancer. The most likely explanation of the lower death rates from cirrhosis, lung complaints, and cancer of the cervix are that church members, especially members of certain churches, have better "health behaviour", they drink less, smoke less, have a better diet, some take more exercise, and they have less promiscuous sex. This may explain why Mormons, Adventists, Amish, orthodox Jews, and clergy of all denominations live longer, 4 years longer for male Adventists. This is not the whole story. Berkman and Syme (1979) found that people lived longer if they had a stronger network of social support, including groups like churches. And there may be a third process, since there are still effects of religion with health behaviour and social support held constant (Broyles and Drenovsky, 1992). This effect is probably due to the peace of mind produced by faith, which may affect the immune system.

(4) Freedom.
Religion can be said to bring "freedom" - from fear of death, from the effects of life stresses, from temptation, sexual desire, and social conventions (Batson et al, 1993). But there are also costs - there is less freedom to question. The latter has been described as "cognitive bondage", and measured by items like "I would feel totally lost without my present religious beliefs" (Batson et al 1993). An early study by Thouless (1935) suggests that rigid thinking may be normal in the sphere of religion. He found that while many of his subjects admitted to being uncertain whether there were tigers in China, they were quite certain that religious propositions were either true or false.

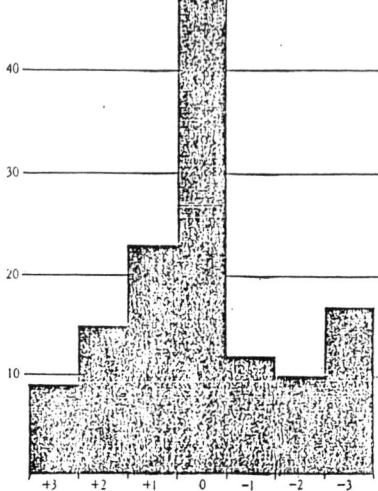

Figure 1a - Tigers are found in parts of China (Thouless 1935)

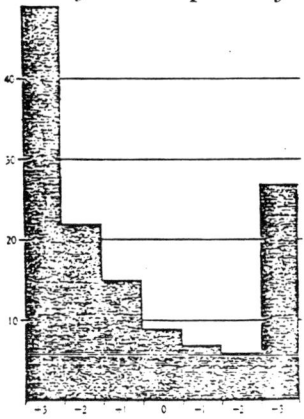

Figure 1b - Jesus Christ was the Son of God (Thouless 1935)

The balance between these two freedoms is different for different religious groups. There has been much concern over a new kind of religion, that of small cults, the "new religious movements". Here there appears to be very little freedom to think, and indeed strict discipline. Some of them have ended in violence and death, as in the Jonesville massacre, the Rajneesh commune in Oregon, and recently at Waco, Texas.

In fundamentalist churches the balance is struck differently. On the positive side we saw that happiness and well-being were greater for those with the most certain beliefs. On the other hand fundamentalists have little freedom to think, and tend to be intolerant and prejudiced towards other groups. This is what psychologists call the "closed mind", associated with cognitive rigidity and authoritarianism (Rokeach, 1960). Non-fundamentalist, more liberal, Christian churches may do less well on certainty, but better on cognitive freedom. Those members who are also high in intrinsic religiosity have the benefits of happiness and mental health; it is also strong predictor of altruism. To do this they have to be non-literal believers, in a metaphorical way, looking for the inexpressible meanings behind the words, which may be found in ritual, music and personal religious experience. Liberal believers are found to be more accepting of psychological research about religion, they can cope with the tension between worldly and other-worldly views of religion, and are able to see beyond the satisfactions which religion gives to the mythical truths behind. Perhaps the test of religious ideas is in their power to transform people, and part of the meaning of beliefs is through their realisation in behaviour (Brown, 1987).

Prosocial behaviour (1) Altruism

A crucial question is whether or not religion actually affects behaviour. Surveys using self-reports of helpfulness, giving money away etc. may be doubted since church members may exaggerate their goodness. Experiments on helping have been more convincing: church members in these experiments have been more willing to read to a blind student, help a lonely girl, go on a charity walk etc., especially the intrinsically religious. Donations to charity, if true, show a strong effect - weekly church attenders in the USA say that they give away about 3.8% of their incomes, while non-attenders give about 0.8%. However this is partly due no doubt to American churches expecting their members to give quite a lot to church funds. The same may happen in Australia where 33% of church members now give 10% of their incomes (Kaldor, 1994). Church members do more voluntary work - an American Gallup poll fund that 46% of those who were "highly spiritually committed" did voluntary work among the "poor, infirm or elderly", compared with 22% for the spiritually uncommitted (Myers, 1993). One of the main explanations people give for doing voluntary work is for religious reasons (Table 4).

Table 4 (Clary and Snyder, 1991)
Percentage of Volunters Reporting Various Reasons for Volunteering: National Surveys[a]

Reasons	1981	1985	1988
Do something useful; help others	45.0	52.0	55.8
Had an interest in activity, working	35.0	36.0	Ni[b]
Enjoy the work; feel needed	29.0	32.0	33.5
Religious concerns	21.0	27.0	21.8
Had someone who was involved in the activity, or would benefit from it	23.0	26.0	27.2
Wanted to learn, get experience; work experience; help get a job	11.0	10.0	9.4
Had a lot of free time	8.0	10.0	8.6
Previously benefited from activity	NI	NI	9.9

a) From the Gallup organisaion's national surveys of volunteering conducted for the Indpendepent Sector in 1981, 1985, 1988 (Gallup organisation, 1986, Independent Sector, 199). The survey items was as follows: "For what reasons did you first become involved in your volunteer activities" and the above reasons were response alternatives. Multiple responses were allowed.
b) NI = question was not included on that year's survey.

The rate of crime is lower for church members, especially for violent crime, with other factors held constant (Petterson, 1991), there is less use of drink and drugs. How much effect there is depends on church rules; the Mormons have very low rates of drinking and smoking for example.

(2) Prejudice and intolerance

This is something of a "sting in the tail", it is a sphere where religion seems to have a bad effect. Although most religions preach love for enemies, this does not always extend to other religious groups. The Inquisition, Moslem fundamentalism, the Crusades, and many "religious" wars have been the result. It has been found in several continents that church members are overall more racially prejudiced than non-members. However this is not true of the intrinsically religious, and it is not true of the most active and committed. Figure 2 shows the results of the a study by Struening (1963), of the racial attitudes of American students.

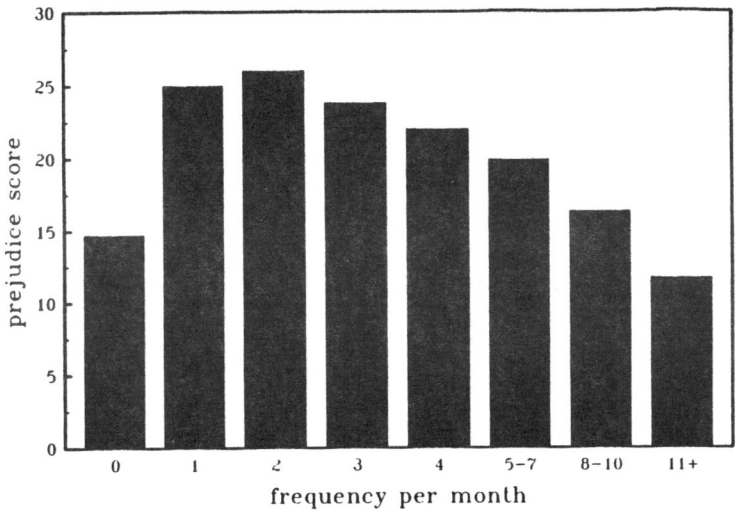

Figure 2 - Prejudice and Church Attendance (Source Struening, 1963)

It can be seen that the most prejudiced were those who went to church 1-3 times a month. It is also found that prejudice is greatest for fundamentalist churches like the American Southern Baptists, and here the most active are the most prejudiced (Wulf, 1991).

It is also found that church members are prejudiced towards members of other churches. Figure 3 shows the results of a study by Rokeach(1960). The vertical scales show the degree of rejection of members of other church, such as not wanting to be friends with them, the horizontal scale shows the other bodies in order of dissimilarity of beliefs.

It can be seen that there is more rejection of members of the churches with different beliefs, and this was strongest for Catholics. There was also a separation of those with "open" and "closed" minds, with different scores on a measure of intolerance. The closed minded rejected other church members more, especially in the cases of Catholics and Baptists.

Conflict between groups is probably the greatest problem in the world to-day; it is ironic that religion should be making this problem worse rather than better.

(3) Sexual behaviour
This is the joke in the tail, but it also raises some fundamental issues. To begin with, churches are generally against sex, in many forms, especially extra-marital, pre-marital and homosexuality. The result is that church members engage in sex less - but not much less. For example for those Americans who describe themselves as "very religious" 71% have had pre-marital intercourse, and 31% have had extra-marital intercourse. Among American Catholics 66% use contraception and 29% of women have had an abortion (Janus and Janus, 1994).

There seems to be a relation between religion and sex, but what exactly is it? Most religions recommend celibacy for the most religious for some reason. Perhaps preventing promiscuity and promoting the integrity of the family is the real goal, though the family does not figure much in the Bible. Is religion in some way a substitute for sex? Sexual restraint may motivate religion, snake handling has been popular in North America (a phallic symbol), and female mystics have reported sexual imagery in their visions.

The rewards and the costs of different kinds of religion
Can we "evaluate" religions or churches on the basis of their psychological fruits? All churches seem to make their members happier, especially the more committed and the older members, partly due to social support, partly to a relation with God, partly because of the benefits of beliefs. We have seen that fundamentalist churches seem to have the greatest effect on the behaviour of their members, and to convey happiness through the certainty of their beliefs. But it is the same churches which impose the greatest loss of cognitive freedom and which are the most intolerant of other social groups and other churches.

For most churches the most committed members are the least prejudiced and the most altruistic. For all churches there are some health benefits, due mainly to better health behaviour and extra social support, but for some churches like the Adventists and Mormons, with strict rules, their members live considerably longer.

For most church members there are gains for mental health, partly due to social support, partly due to a supportive religion with God and the practice of religious coping, but revivals and some fanatical cults can have a negative effect.

However the relation between psychology and religion has so far scarcely been explored at all, and it could be an immense enterprise, to which this chapter is just the beginning.

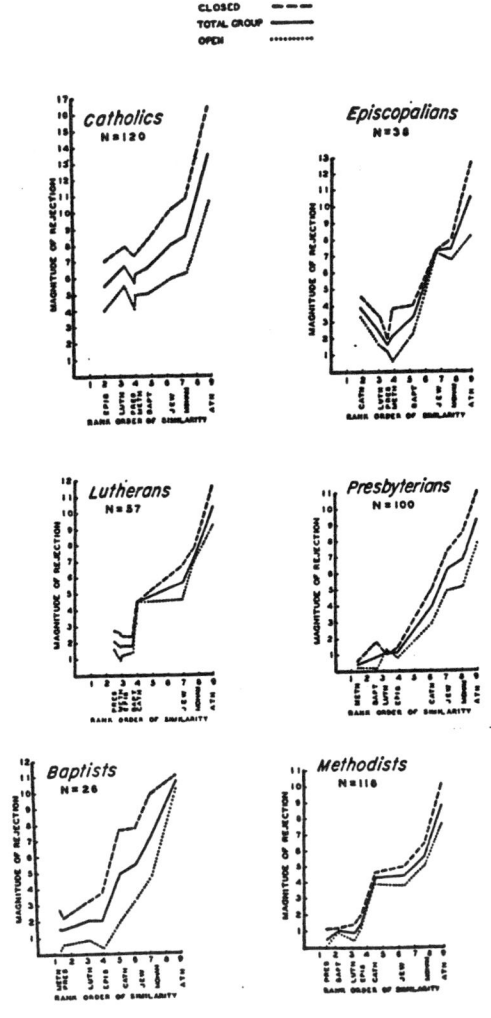

Figure 3

References

Argyle, M. (in press) Psychology and Leisure. London: Penguin Books.
Argyle, M. and Beit-Hallahmi, B. (1975) The Social Psychology of Religion. London: Routledge and Kegan Paul.
Batson, C.D., Schoenrade, P. and Ventis, W.L. (1993) Religion and the Individual. New York: Oxford University Press.
Beit-Hallahmi, B.,Bronw, L.B. and Argyle, M. (in press) Religious Behaviour, Beliefs and Experience. London: Routledge and Kegan Paul.
Berger, P.L. and Luckmann, T. (1966) The Social Construction of Reality. Garden City, NY: Doubleday.
Berkman,,L.F. and Syme,S.L. (1979) Social networks, host resistance, and mortality: a nine year follow-up study of Alameda county residents. American Journal of Epidemiology,109,186-204.
Brown, L.B. (1987) The Psychology of Religious Belief. London: Academic Press.
Broyles, P.A. and Drenovsky, C.K. (1992) Religious attendance the subjective health of the elderly. Review of Religious Research, 34,152-160.
Chamberlain,K. and Zika,S. (1988) Religiosity, life meaning, and well-being. Journal for the Scientific Study of Religion,27,411-420.
Clary,E.G. and Snyder, M.(1991) A functional analysis of altruism and prosocial behaviour: the case of volunteerism in M.S. Clark (ed) Prosocial Behaviour. Newbury Park: Sage.
Comstock,G.W. and Partridge,K.B. (1972) Church attendance and health. Journal of Chronic Diseases,25,665-672.
Csikszentmihalyi,M. (1975) Beyond Boredom and Anxiety. San Francisco: Jossey-Bass.
Dwyer,J.W., Clarke,L.L., and Miller,M.K. (1990) The effect of religious concentration and affiliation on county cancer mortality rates. Journal of Health and Social Behaviour, 31,185-202.
Gray,J. (1987) The mind-brain identity as a scientific hypothesis: a second look.in C.Blakemore and S.Greenfield (eds) Mindwaves, Oxford: Blackwell. University Press.
Janus,S.S. and Janus, C.L. (1993) The Janus Report, New York: Wiley
Kaldor,P. (1994) Winds of Change. Homebush West, NSW: Anzea Publishers.

Lewis,L.R. and Bromley, D.G. (1987) The cult withdrawal syndrome: a case of misattribution of cause? Journal for the Scientific Study of Religion, 26,508-522.

Marcel,A.J. and Bisiach,E.eds. (1988) Consciousness in Contemporary Science. Oxford: Clarendon Press.

Moberg, D.O. and Taves, M.J. (1965) Church participation and adjustment in old age.in A.M.Rose and W.A. Peterson (eds) Older People and their Social World. Philadelphia: F.A. Davis.

Myers,D.G. (1992) The Pursuit of Happiness. New York: W.Morrow.

Pargament,K.I.,et al (1988) Religion and the problem-solving process: three styles of coping. Journal for the Scientific Study of Religion, 27,90-104.

Penrose,R.(1989) The Emperor's New Mind. Oxford: Oxford University Press.

Pollner, M. (1989) Divine relations, social relations, and well-being. Journal of Health and Social Behaviour, 30,92-104

Rokeach,M. (1960) The Open and Closed Mind. New York: Basic Books.

Petterson,T.(1991) Religion and criminality: structural relations between church involvement and crime rates in contemporary Sweden. Journal for the Scientific Study of Religion. 30,279-291.

Searle,J.(1984) Minds, Brains and Science. London: BBC.

Struening,E.L. (1963) Anti-democratic attitudes in Midwest University. in H.H.,Remmers (ed) Antidemocratic Attitudes in American Schools. Evanston,Ill.: Northwestern University Press.

Thouless,R.H. (1935) The tendency towards certainty in religious beliefs. British Journal of Psychology, 26,16-31

Wulf,D.M. (1991) Psychology of Religion. New York: Wiley.

The experience of sadness
Rev. Dr. Neville Stewart

It is an enormous challenge to try to relate to one of the great themes of human existence. One thinks of Shakespeare and Job. On first being asked I refused for a variety of reasons. I was then led to think again and I agreed. Great figures can make their contribution but there is also a place for an ordinary person seeking to share the experience and meaning of something which is universal. Since most of us are ordinary (though unique and hence special, wonderful in our uniqueness) perhaps this contribution will be complementary to those from the more extraordinary sources. So this is a whole person sharing by one member of the human family with others of that same family for the purpose of mutual enlightenment, enrichment. It is not a lecture or a sermon, though it may have aspects of both. I am encouraged to recall that all good "didache", the Greek for teaching, is also "kerygma", proclamation and vice-versa. Hopefully it will be a dialogue, two-way, inter-active rather than one-way, passive whether you hear or read.

Personal Background
So what of the person who is engaging in this whole-person sharing exercise? A few indicators may assist in the context of the Christ and the Cosmos Initiative exploring the religion/science interface. From the age of 14 I specialised in science, finally focusing on chemistry. Following graduation I worked as an analytical chemist. This has left an indelible mark, not so much in terms of factual content but in approach, methodology. I am incurably analytic! Having ceased the practice of science I have continued my interest in a scientific approach to being and doing. Being faced with the hypothesis that I should offer as a Methodist minister, I put it to the test via a variety of means including rational though, dialogue with others and myself, prayer, bible study, whole-person reflection, intuition, examining tradition. I concluded the hypothesis was sound. Having begun in faith I continued in faith, as all science does,

and finding my offer accepted I entered the "alien" worlds of theology and philosophy. Having not written an essay since the age of 14, I struggled but gradually I came to see that science, theology, philosophy are aspects of one truth, better put as one truth who is God seen especially through and in Jesus. This conviction has remained. I have been often puzzled, deeply challenged but have always felt the presence of a basic congruity. Life is a continuous process of revelation/whole person reaction received in faith and worked out by faith.

I have academic qualifications in Science, Theology/Philosophy and management studies but not in Psychology! So what qualified me to speak in this particular content? It is possible to gain a working familiarity with a field without having a degree and that I have done, especially via my long involvement in education. How, why, when, where people learn, for example, were persistent questions to which Psychology provides many answers. But whilst It is true a little knowledge can be dangerous and the praxis of academia is necessary and desirable, it will be sad day when in order to address an area one must first have an academic qualification. I am also encouraged by the experience of meeting people with cartloads of qualifications but who seem neither wise nor useful! We are in danger of finding ourselves retreating into increasingly rarefied specialisms with their own language, immigration police etc. producing an alarmed, dis-integrated existence. We need constantly to affirm and explore our common humanity, members one of another, and share, explain, illuminate each other in the light of our various specialisms. Perhaps foremost in my "qualifications" is that from 1992-4 I was severely ill with M.E. and depression. This was an experience of sadness at a depth far greater than anything previous. Since recovering I have tried to analyse what happened to me so that I can learn from the experience. A long-standing involvement in holistic health recovery and maintenance now occupies much of my time working in the field of counselling, spirituality and stress management. In particular, having been a meditator for many years and found it especially helpful during my illness, I now run a meditation group and teach relaxation, breathing, body awareness, focusing, imaging, contemplation.

Key concepts in the perspective

These are holistic/whole person, inter-connection, inter-dependency, integrated systems. The paradox of the one and the many, the part and the whole is of perennial importance, not least in our times when the culture of privatised greed, the 'I' generation is widespread and where in the world of health there is so much exclusive stress on the "material" rather than seeing it as part of the complex, integrated system. It is vital we have a both and approach as through the theme of the Conference, members one of another. Nowhere is this integrated approach more needed than in the world of the so-called disciplines and especially in the science and the rest divide. It is a long time since C.P. Snow raised the issue of the two cultures and asserted it was artificial and unsustainable. We have yet o hear and accept. For example if, amongst many other things, science is the exercise of holistic, creative imagination via applied models/images, relating to energies of which love is the basic energy all in the context of faith it is interesting to compare it with work in the fields of art, music, literature and many other areas.
So this is an attempt to speak of sadness in a holistic way, perhaps more of a helicopter view but having a micro as well as a macro approach.

I have maintained we are complex, wonderful integrated systems. I want us to look at the some of the parts which go to make up the whole. We can only really start to get a proper perspective on sadness in this context. There are many ways of expressing reality via models. They are all inadequate and distant to a degree. But just as geographic map is limited and to a degree distorting yet enabling us to have a wider view of the territory, so hopefully these maps will do the same.

A holistic word map as the context for sadness

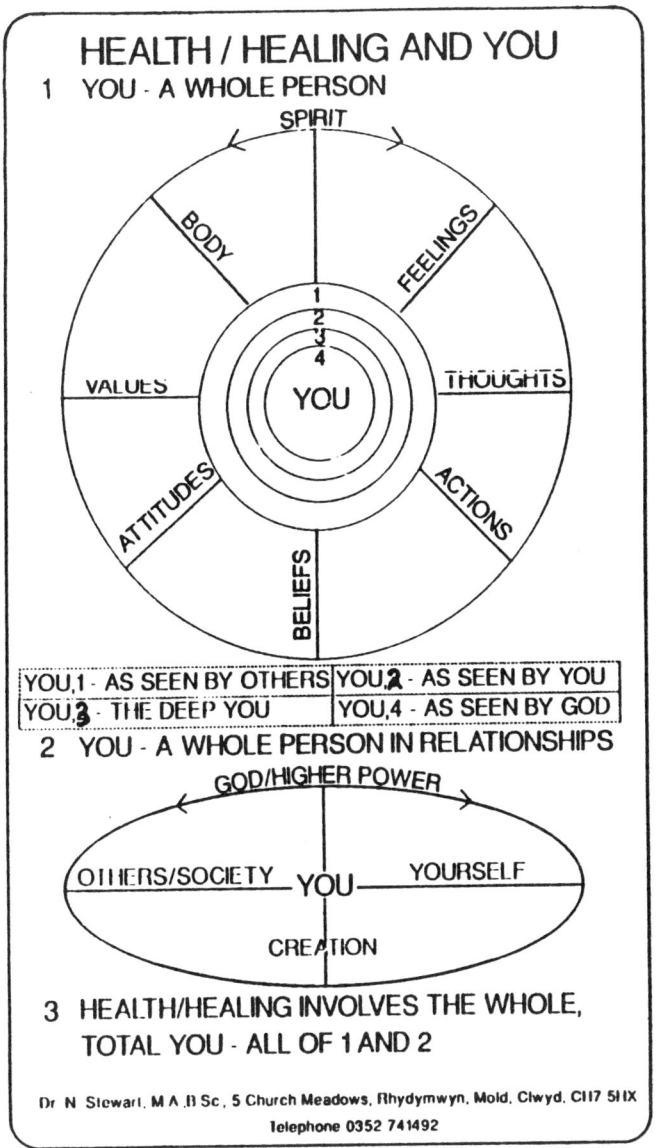

Map 1
The 1,2,3,4 concentric circles remind us of the many "layers" of what we are as persons. The "layers" are not like those of an onion. They are more like ingredients all inter-acting together to make the "cake". But that is a static model and being a person is a process where the many ingredients are constantly reacting. In a real sense we are new every moment. The four "layers" given an outline overview of the main headings, each immensely complex within themselves and in relation to each other. We are constantly aware of and reacting to the fact of our perception of how others are perceiving us. Then we are aware of a conscious sense of identity, I am me. Psychology as much as any other discipline has made us more aware that our conscious awareness is only the small tip of a large iceberg which is our unconscious self. Everything that has happened to us from conception, and some would say before, is stored within us, not always easy to access but having a profound influence. The deep you is very much a reality. Then most powerful and comprehensive of all is our relationship with God. It is God in whom we live and move and have our being. As Paul said, for me to live is Christ: I live yet not I but Christ lives in me. Or John who speaks of the indwelling spirit and uses the model of the vine and the branches, mutual abiding. It is helpful to identify main aspects that go to the making of a person. We shall leave feelings for special attention later. It is vital to stress that these so-called separate aspects are all inseparable parts of a dynamic process that operates as a totally integrated system. It is useful to look at, say, feelings as separate entity only so long as we remember that in practice feelings are only a part of this integrated system, constantly affected and affecting. So, briefly, let us take a helicopter view of the territory.
<u>Thoughts</u> We are what we think, though as we shall see later cognition is not the unique and dominant facet many have maintained. Nevertheless, we are what we think. The field of holistic or "min/body" medicine gives powerful examples. Those cancer patients who think positively about their illness are more likely to live longer. The phenomenon of the placebo continues to

amaze. If we think a tablet will have a certain effect it is more likely it will irrespective of the composition. For more on this whole field see for example Moyers, Healing and the Mind: Doubleday; The Healing Brain, Ornstein & Sobell, Macmillan; Get Well Again: Simantan, Bantam or any of the books by Bernie Siegel. Whether you are dominantly positive or negative in your thinking matters greatly.

<u>Actions</u> We are what we do. As Jesus said, by their fruits you shall know them. In the parable of the sheep and the goats it is deeds that are the criterion of judgement. The smallest difference in our actions has an effect both on ourselves and others. For example scowling and smiling give a measurably different neural reaction on the skin of the arm, affecting our personal integrated system as well as others around us.

<u>Beliefs</u> We are what we believe. Our beliefs have a powerful, all pervading influence. It does matter, profoundly what we believe. If, as I believe(!), we live by faith then the only option open to us is to choose what we believe in, who and what we trust. At the relatively trivial level, people given a particular pack of cards and asked to find the ace of clubs were largely unsuccessful. They believed the ace of clubs was black whereas in this pack it was red. At the more profound level, studies of those subject to torture, interrogation, solitary confinement show that those with the greatest faith withstand the best and are the hardest to break down.

<u>Attitudes</u> We are what we attitudinise. An attitude is a dominant disposition, contributed to by other facets of our personality and experience! We can see this clearly in the areas of race and gender. We all have basic attitude in these and other similar areas. As the result again of a variety of factors such as upbringing we can have predominantly closed or open attitudes to things and predominantly trustful or mistrustful attitudes to others . Irrespective of the details of genetic inheritance and environmental, nurturing experience, we all have a range of attitudes which influence powerfully who and what we are, all the more powerful for being again largely not operating at the conscious level.

<u>Values</u> We are what we value. Our values are what in practice we deem to be of supreme importance. In many ways there are our gods of which we usually have a pantheon in hierarchical form. We can value food, sport, sea, pleasure, power, money, people. An analysis of what dominates our time, our secret desires, our imagination, our dreams often gives a clear idea of our values. A Christian seeks to value God supremely, to lover Her/Him, expressing it through love for neighbour and self and seeing all else in that context.

<u>Body</u> We are, for instance, what we eat. Each person is a unique, complex chemical, neural system using the same materials and processes of which the stars are made. We are incredibly amazing chemical producers on a continuous process basis, sustaining our physical existence. Our physical, material systems are integrated with all our other systems. Fear can make our pulse race, embarrassment our cheeks blush. Our breathing powerfully affects our whole being in much more than a chemical sense. The familiar attitudes of either worshipping the body as such e.g. male/female models or denigrating it as part of a lower/evil system e.g. much of our attitude towards sex, are equally erroneous. The physical body is an integral part of our feelings, attitudes etc. It does matter what we eat for more than physical health reasons. The body is the temple of the Spirit but is not just the superstructure rather an integral part of the system itself. The brain is not just what is in our heads but, for example, is structurally connected chemically and neurally to every one of the millions of cells in our system.

<u>Spirit</u> We are spiritual beings, made in the image of God. the spirit is what we essentially are via our being/doing. Finally it is mysterious but not surprisingly. What in reality is totally explainable? So much in science is ultimately mysterious, as evidenced by the way myths are accompanying maths. Who has seen, fully understands a quark? So much physical science works on the same basis as John describing the Holy Spirit: we don't know hat/who it is, where it comes from, where it goes but we experience the effect. Person as spirit is the result of synergy, the interaction of the various parts whereby the sum is much more than the parts added

together. We call that mysterious, fully experienced reality a person, a spiritual being.

Map 2
Here we see that no person exits in isolation. We are literally members one of another, e.g. the way we share, have the loan of, chemicals from the common store of the created universe which go to make up our physical body for a time, then revert back to the common store - ashes to ashes, dust to dust. We are always persons in relationship. Our ancestors are alive in us in a variety of ways. At the day to day level we are bound up in a continuous, dynamic network of relationships. We relate to ourselves; to especially significant, others; to the physical creation, environment; above all we relate to God both as a particular entity and as Someone who is intimately connected with all other aspects of being/doing. Jesus summed it up in terms of loving God/neighbour/self.
We need to see our Western culture in the light of this holistic context. There are grievous aberrations, distortions with horrendous results. Three brief illustrations from politics, medicine and religion. In politics we have heard Margaret Thatcher say there is no such thing as society, only individuals, a position which informs so much of the privatisation, "personal greed is in" culture. The disastrous consequences are tragically visible all around us. Our medical world tends to be dominated by cuts, chemicals and technology. They are vital and powerful but limited. Health, sickness relates to the whole of the two maps. More than 50% of people visiting their GP's have a problem predominantly non-physical. They go largely untreated except at the level of a chemical prescription to help with relieving symptoms rather than dealing with courses. Our religious world tends to other extremes. We are obsessed with the verbal/rational. So we have problems with meditation and silent prayer, especially in our Methodist culture. We have problems coming to terms with sex and sexuality and accepting that Jesus was for real as a human person, probably seen more clearly via a bottom-up rather than a top-down approach. Much christology, until recently, has tended to

be docetic, denying the reality of the incarnation, the Word became flesh, and the crucifixion. To confuse things many want the Risen Jesus to be physically real and castigate those who have problems with this approach as denying the fact of the Resurrection.
My heartfelt plea is for a holistic approach across the whole of life. Health, wholeness, shalom, salvation are words having a common root. They describe a complex, dynamic process having many interconnected parts making a total integrated system. The significance of the part can only be seen in the context of the whole. Similarly the whole can only be understood in the light of the multitudinous parts. Salvation, health involves keeping this total system in overall harmony and balance to enable the achieving of the purposes of love. It is in this context that we must see the concept of sadness.
Before proceeding to look at feelings in particular, I invite you to form into groups of three and to discuss, with each contributing, when did you last cry, why, how did you feel and what did you make of the experience. If you can't, won't, don't cry then discuss why.

Feelings: Descartes' Error
When considering the first Word Map we noted feeling but left it for later consideration. In early 1995 Antonio Damasio, an American doctor, professor at Iowa State University and one of the world's leading neurologist, published a similar book, the result of long and copious research, called Descartes' Error: Emotion, Reason and the Human Brain. From the point of view of a neuro-biologist, he challenges Descartes' profoundly influential "I think, therefore I am". Since I have spent many years issuing the same challenge from philosophical, theological and other perspectives, an American professor friend sent me a copy. It is impossible in so short a space to enter into the immense and fascinating detail of the book, but the main thesis is clear. From the perspective of a neuro-biologist he maintains Descartes was in error on at least three counts:
1. He should have recognised the person as a total system, bigger than any of the parts, and said "I am, therefore I think."

2. He gave primacy to the rational function of the brain. Damasio shows that the brain is itself a total modular system within a total system. The most basic power and function, as we have evolved, lies not with the module concerned with cognition but with the module concerned with emotion. Descartes should have said, and in the light of what we now know about the brain we should say "I am, therefore I feel and can thus interpret thought, predict the consequences of action and make effective choices." This merits long and careful pondering as it has major theoretical and practical implications for the way we live and operate.
3. He maintained there is a site in the brain/person where the mind reigns supreme, the sources of the mind/body dualism responsible for so much error and disaster e.g. in the field of sex and sexuality. The brain is a complex modular system with modules more or less relating to particular functions such as cognition, emotion. As stated in 2. if there is one module more basic than any other it is that relating to emotion and the fusing of emotion and cognition, not that relating to cognition alone. The unique, wonderful, conscious "I" arises from the co-operative, coherent activity of neurous in many brain modules.

Accepting Damasio's position, which I do on scientific and other grounds, means in many ways a Copernican revolution with the most far-reaching consequences. There is space for only two examples :

a) Decision making. This is predominantly seen as a rational action where emotion is suppressed, ignored or at best removed. Good decisions come from cool, calm, collected rational consideration of the facts. It just does not work like that. We can only ever have a tiny fraction of the factual information relative to any particular decision. What in fact we do when making decisions is to be massively selective in the facts we use: we cannot do otherwise remembering the near unlimited factual resource and the need to actually decide. We are equally selective in the areas that we choose to ignore. If it is a technical decision relating to a computer system we are very likely to ignore facts from sociology, psychology, theology etc. Again how could it be otherwise if we are ever to decide, though someone at some stage needs to take a total view. When we then pause to remember that so-called pure "facts" are illusion and are all value, emotion laden, the illusion of the model is seen more clearly. Yes, we need "facts" but we need to recall their status and limited availability in practice. But if the "pure facts" scenario is an illusion, how much more is that of the emotionless, pure rationality model of decision-making. Emotion always plays a major part in every decision, at least and usually more significant than the rational/factual component. Hence instead of denying, suppressing, ignoring emotion we should pay at least as much attention to it as other components. The question to ask is not whether emotion plays a part but what emotions are appropriate for what decisions. It would seem that for some decisions anger is appropriate and necessary. Anger played a key role when Jesus invaded the temple and overturned the tables of the money-changers. Gut feeling, intuition with emotion a key component is basic to decision making.

b) Scientific discovery. The typical picture is of desiccated calculating machines, high powered cerebral activity particularly mathematical. Of course such cerebral activity has a vital place but it is only part of the picture. It needs to be remembered that beauty, form and symmetry have a significant role in mathematics and it is a role engaging predominantly those parts of the brain most concerned with emotion. The history of scientific discovery tells a continuing story of hunches, intuition, creative imagination, emotion all tied in with often grinding experimentation and rational activity. The discovery of the benzene ring structure in organic chemistry spent endless hours in the laboratory but the structure finally came to him when he fell asleep on a journey and dreamt of a snake swallowing its tail!

We need, then, to accept the primacy of feelings. This will involve a radical change from the dominantly negative, fearful, dismissive view of feelings in our culture. This can take a variety of forms.

1. **Denial.** I am feeling dreadful. A friend says "How are you?" I respond with "I'm feeling fine". Denial can be a useful safety-valve while we adjust to say bad news received. It is when we continue the denial after the initial phase that we store up trouble. How often have men in particular denied feelings of grief and fought back tears at funerals.
2. **Rejection.** This is close to denial and can be the result of persistent denial. The Stoics thought it a virtue to reject emotion giving the impression of being emotionally impregnable whatever the circumstances. Many still follow this disastrous path.
3. **Suppression.** This is another variation on the negative theme. Yes, I have deep feelings but I never accept, show them but keep them safely out of sight under secure lock and key.
4. **Repression.** the denied, rejected, suppressed emotions go underground, beneath the conscious level but still enormously powerful and often evident in our dreams. The child who represses feelings of anger can grow up into an adult monster.
5. **Mindless surrender.** Perhaps as a reaction to 1-4, this goes to the other extreme. "Why did you beat the man to death?" "I felt like doing it". Whatever I feel like I must express. Feelings reign supreme, nothing else matters. Dr. Spock has now repented of his teachings whereby parents were advised to always allow children to give full vent to their feelings whatever the consequences. He now speaks of tough love. In another realm a high powered, highly placed female advertising executive in an interview gloried in her emotional tantrums in dealing with staff. "I'm a shit and I want everyone to know it".

Feelings are basic, the basic ingredient in the total system. Because they are basic, powerful all the more reason for working in balance, harmony, appropriateness and above all seeking the guidance of the Spirit at all times. Jesus in Gethsemane is perhaps the classic illustration of the deepest emotions at work, with struggle and tension beyond our comprehension. But the first, ongoing and final word was that of the Spirit enabling the obedient acceptance of love.

Sadness

We have considered the person as a holistically integrated, total system with feelings playing a major part. Now we turn to sadness. First I invite you to listen to some music. Music can communicate powerfully with those parts of the brain concerned with emotion as well as cognition. I shall play a recording of the aria in Bach's St. Matthew's Passion where Peter, having denied Jesus, expresses his sadness. The text is a prayer "Have mercy, Lord, on me. Regard my bitter weeping: Look on me: Heart and eyes both weep to thee bitterly."

Sadness is overwhelmingly the reaction of our system to loss. It does not only affect our feelings but it is there I wish to put the main focus.

Sadness covers the widest spectrum. At one end I can feel sad because my team have lost in the Cup Final. Further along the spectrum is something much stronger. The Americans have labelled it dysthymia - you have to have a mysterious, preferably Greek label, for something to be real! This is when life is overwhelmingly colourless, you always feel more down than up, there is little joy and hope and feelings often border on despair. Concentration is poor, you are often gloomy and irritable. You either sleep to little or too much, eat too little or too much. It has been shown dysthymia is very widespread. At the far end of the spectrum is severe depression. I suffered from a long period of severe depression during the two years from 1992 to 1994 when I was extremely ill with M.E. On of the reasons why I finally agreed to give this paper and include a personal reference was to say that sadness, depression can happen to anyone, Christian, minister, anyone. We need to be much more open in accepting this. We accept without stigma that anyone can have heart trouble and this brings out sympathy in most people. Would that the same sympathy, compassion could be there when depression and sickness of the mind and spirit are concerned, though I was fortunate. At its worst, depression is indescribably terrible. Words hardly begin to convey the experience. In my case I suffered severe loss of health, energy, purpose. I could hardly read, think, converse for long periods. I couldn't manage my affairs. A friend took over things like tax returns. I didn't handle money for over a year. I was so weak that my wife had to cut up my food for me. I felt useless, a burden, worthless. Life became increasingly meaningless with no hope, no way forward. I was persuaded I was going to finish up a mad cabbage. I thought of suicide but never actively contemplated it. Increasingly I felt isolated yet when visitors arrived I tended to recoil and reject. Time was a great enemy and I vividly recall living from one ten minutes to the next ..... if I can manage the next ten minutes .... Four a.m. to eight a.m. was the daily time of mental torture which then soon turned into morning after morning of endless sobbing. It seemed as if I was at the bottom of a dark, slimy pit with no way up or out. I had lost much of what constituted life previously resulting in unutterable sadness.

Sadness, though not severe depression, is normal to the human condition. It is vital we accept this. Taking Jesus as the supreme example of normality we note that He experienced sadness. He wept over the death of Lazarus, His friend. He wept over Jerusalem. The looming loss of life and the horror of crucifixion produced the profound sadness of Gethsemane. On the cross, the cry of dereliction "My God, My God why have you forsaken me" reveals all the emotion resulting from the seeming loss of God. Sadness is normal because overwhelmingly it results from loss and life is a process of loss and gain, of death and resurrection. When we are born we lose the safety of the womb and are catapulted into a very different world. The process continues. When a child goes to school there are often tears of sadness, the child losing the regular presence of the mother and vice-versa. But always there is gain. We lose the innocence of childhood, the freedom of adolescence. Friendship and marriage are made up of loss and gain. Nearly always there is sadness mixed with other emotions. So the pattern continues. Many suffer loss and sadness through divorce, redundancy, bereavement. We face the crisis of middle-age and even more so old age. Again there is loss in a variety of ways and sadness. But all can be gain.

The final loss is that of life itself but out of death comes resurrections.

Forces causing sadness can be internal or external, endogenous or reactive. There are useful categories but in the end they are inseparable.

<u>Dealing with sadness</u>
A great deal has been written and much is known that is helpful. This is not the occasion for detailed guidance. I can though share with you an analytical took which came out of my own experience and which is applicable to sadness and many other situations. It is ASCOTS and has nothing to do with horse-racing!

Acceptance. It is essential that we accept positively reality as it presents itself form moment to moment. That is so easy to say, sometimes so hard to do yet always a vital essential. The first stage in dealing with sadness is to accept the situation as it is, always positively and with hope. It is significant that the word resignation has come to have a negative meaning. It used to signify positive acceptance. It is the Pauline experience "In whatsoever state I am, therein to be content". For Christians there is always and everywhere hope. It took me nine months to accept that I was ill in spite of the evidence and that acceptance played a key part in my recovery.

Survival. There are times when it is bare survival, just existing, living from hour to hour. The good news is that nearly always these periods to pass. We need to learn survival techniques.

Coping. This is when we are managing reasonably. After periods of surviving it seems like bliss. But we can get beyond coping.

Overcoming. This is when we have really come to terms with things, we are on top of the situation.

Transforming. This is when we see the whole situation in a new, positive, larger content, the realisation that all things work together for good to those who love God.

Service. His fortune, loss, sadness leave us wide open to the temptation to self-pity and other forms of selfishness. A major antidote is service, doing things for others, losing in order to find. It is always possible. A totally paralysed lady, except for eye movement, caused by polio, went through all the stages, finishing dominantly in the S section. She learnt to use a computer via eye movement in order to write letters to people in trouble.
It is instructive to apply the ASCOTS formula to the life and death of Jesus. It needs time, concentration and imagination but will give much dividends in terms of transforming sadness, leading to the realisation that sadness/joy are the head and tail of the same coin.

Using, learning from sadness
The ASCOTS formula can show us how to transform sadness. This does not mean we avoid the pain. George Matheson gave us the great hymn "O Love That Wilt Not Let Me Go", including the line "O joy that seekest me through pain". This hymn came out of his own deep experience of loss and sadness. He lost his sight and then the woman he loved as a result. But through and out of the sadness came joy.
It is my experience that nothing, not even the severest of depressions, can separate us from the love of God. I had often read and quoted from Psalm 139, "If I descend into hell you are there". I now know from deep personal experience it is true. In the midst of all the despair, loss, darkness, meaninglessness paradoxically there was a mysterious source of not being alone, of being held. Dora Greenwell had a motto on all her books, "I hold and I am held". The holding, our faith, is important but nowhere near so vital as being held. Ultimately all is grace. Perhaps the words which mediated this most to me and which I repeated endlessly are from Isaiah 43:1 and 2. I always put my name first to make it a personal address:
> "Neville, do not be afraid for I have set you free: I have called you by name, you are mine. When you pass through the waters I will be with you: and through the rivers they shall not

overwhelm you: when you walk through the fire you shall not be burned and the flame shall not consume you".
Life can indeed be resurrection now, as Harry Williams puts it in True Resurrection.

Carers
This relates to all of us because to a greater or lesser degree we are all called to care for each other, especially in items of loss and sadness. It is important to understand, sympathise, empathise and exercise endless patience. The "pull yourself together, snap out of it" approach can be cruelly inappropriate, though there is need for such as self-pity to be challenged. Encouragement, affirmation are essential. When a person feels deep despair, worthlessness, finding it hard to love oneself, it is all the more vital that others build up and share their love, in words as well as deeds. Often simply being there is crucial. Touch can be powerful, re-assuring and healing. When the sadness of depression is deep, the urge, capacity to communicate by speech and gesture all but vanishes. One such sufferer was regularly visited by a friend who recognised his condition and simply massaged his feet. The role of carer is to be there in love, ready and willing to respond sensitively as different needs arise.

The Emmaus road story (Luke 2-4) Jesus and two travellers: a case study of Jesus dealing with sad clients.
I invite you to read the story three times. First, read it in the normal way. Then read it again more slowly, lingering over scenes and phrases. Then close your eyes and relive the story in your imagination. Let it speak to the whole of you.
We are used to using titles such as Lord, Saviour for Jesus. Try now the title Counsellor and see the two travellers as His clients.
The two travellers were extremely sad, suffering from supreme loss. Jesus had been crucified; He was gone and so cruelly. All had been focused on Him. "We had hoped He would redeem Israel". Their world had collapsed, despair, hopelessness, sadness had taken over. There had been rumours of Jesus resurrected but they discounted

them. Their sadness was too deep for them to hear. So they were retreating, mechanically, back home, back to the womb, in a thick , one mechanical step after another. Having failed to accept the early news of the resurrection, all they could do was to survive, stage two of ASCOTS.

Then in a mysterious but real way they find a stranger walking with them. Perhaps here we may put the whole story in context. How much is history? Was there such a real even and if so what did the early church make of it, how was it shaped? Is it the product of Luke's or some other's, creative imagination? These are important and legitimate questions to which we must all formulate working answers. I am reminded of the physicist watching a magnificent sunset. He had many scientific questions and observations but he also was overwhelmed by the sheer beauty of the scene. I can only say the Emmaus Road story rings true for me, authenticated by so many other parallel experiences in my life and millions of others. Life so much of the Gospels it would seem there is a historical core plus the creative, Spirit led, imagination of others. God forbid we should fail to appreciate the truth at the heart of the story. A reverent agnosticism about some things need not extinguish the fire of faith.

So the mysterious stranger draws alongside and joins them on their journey. He empathises with them, feels their sadness and invites them to tell Him their story. They now stand still. We can see them with heads down, hunched shoulders, their body language speaking powerfully of their despairing sadness. They are still capable of anger. The kind enquiry of the stranger is met by a beast, a torrent of words releasing pent-up feelings. "Haven't you heard ...." The Stranger listens, surely understands and then responds. The response is no mealy-mouthed set of platitudes. The Stranger would not have qualified or been accepted by the many so-called non-directive schools of counselling. He clearly recognised non-directiveness to be an illusion, however vital it is to listen and let the client tell her story and own solutions. The Stranger challenges them with very strong language. They must have been shaken rigid to have called

"fools, slow of heart". He is challenging them to accept a new Reality, putting things in a new context. They listen, perhaps moving slowly to the coping stage.
They reach Emmaus. The Stranger makes as if to go on. He meets and shares and lifts but never invades. "Behold I stand at the door and knock ....". The travellers are breaking out of their despair. The Stranger offers hope. they invite Him to stay with them, to come in to their dwelling-pace. As ever, He accepts. Now they are moving to the overcoming stage. They sit down for a meal. The Stranger breaks the bread and at that moment they know Him for who He is, Jesus, risen, alive. And then He disappears, leaving them excited, hopeful, the start of transformation. He has again gone, left them but this time they are not sad. They recall how they felt as He talked with them on the journey. "Did not our hearts burn within us". The fire of new hope, new joy was starting to burn in their lives. It brings a new energy. From being downcast, dispirited, tired from physical, psychological, spiritual exhaustion they have a new dynamic. They don't even stay for a rest. This is a new vision and using their new energy they immediately start back on the long journey to Jerusalem. This time shoulders are back, heads high, a spring in the step, joy in their hearts. This is the start of the serving, sharing stage. They have good news but they do not, selfishly keep it to themselves. They are impelled to share it.
They get to Jerusalem, ready to blurt out their incredible discovery, their unbelievable good news. They discover they do not have an exclusive. Jesus, the Stranger, has already appeared to Peter. Excitedly they exchange their good news stories and the joy heightens and heightens. Then, incredibly, Jesus again appears. Initially they are afraid. They are still working through the accepting, transforming experience. It is not like flicking a switch. Jesus asks them why they are still troubled, sad. He shows them His hands and His feet. The wounds are still there, symbols of sadness turned to joy, despair to hope, darkness to light, resurrection in death. There is no ultimate loss, all is gain: no ultimate sadness, all is

joy. Death is taken and transformed. No wonder they "disbelieved for joy".

"Then I saw a new heaven and new earth: for the first heaven and the first earth had passed away and the sea was nor more. And I saw the holy city, new Jerusalem, coming down out of heaven from God, prepared as a bride adorned for her husband: and I heard a great voice from the throne saying, "Behold the dwelling of God is with men. He will dwell with them and they shall be his people and God himself will be with them: he will wipe away every tear from their eyes, and death shall be no more, neither shall there be mourning nor crying nor pain any more, for the former things have passed away. And he who sat upon the throne said "Behold I am making all things new". Indeed He is. The Emmaus travellers experience can be ours as He takes our sadness and transforms it into joy unspeakable.

THE PSYCHO-DYNAMICS OF LIFE AND WORSHIP

Rev. Dr. Bruce Reed

Contents

Introduction .... Page 75
    Dynamics of Life .... Page 75
    Regression to Dependence .... Page 76
    Oscillation .... Page 82
Working Hypothesis .... Page 84
Analysis of Oscillation Process .... Page 88
    Realisation Mode .... Page 89
    Regression Mode .... Page 92
    Identification Mode .... Page 97
    Transformation Mode .... Page 101
To Sum Up .... Page 104

INTRODUCTION

I wish to introduce the theme of this Consultation - *Members One of Another* by referring to three happenings which have come as disclosures to me in succession over the years.

Dynamics of Life

The first occurred when I was a young student of architecture at the University of Melbourne. It was an exciting and creative period in opening up doors into many civilisations and their manners of life as expressed through their artforms, buildings and the ways they planned their cities, towns and villages. In the course of our studies we attended a lecture by a Jewish Rabbi. I had never heard a Jew speak about his faith before, and as someone who considered himself a Christian I was interested in what he had to say about his religion. His introductory words gave me a shock, the waves of which have reverberated in me ever since. He said "the Hebrews had no word for **religion**, they spoke of **life**." For them God, people and the world were all one, and any one aspect could not be addressed without all the others. My idea that as a Christian, I had to learn about my faith, then learn to apply it, was shaken to the core - **what my life was, was** my faith - there was not one phase of being a Christian to be followed by how to apply it in the world during the other aspects of my life.

If life is given by God, then to understand life involves understanding its relation to God at all points. To think on this basis '**religiously**' is to relate God only to apart of life, leaving it open as to how far it penetrates or expands into the remainder. A person who sees themselves as religious becomes one who is associated with God in a way which implies that he or she is subtracting themselves from a full life, not necessarily adding something to the whole.

What I want to discuss this evening is **life**. Looking back I see how easy it is to trip up. I called my book on this topic not '*The Dynamics of Life*' but '*The Dynamics of Religion*'![1]

---

[1] Bruce D Reed **The Dynamics of Religion** London: DLT (1978) This lecture is a revision of the oscillation theory using different terms to describe it.

Regression to Dependence

The second encounter was some years later in London. I was closely involved with the Tavistock Institute in studying human behaviour in groups and institutions. In carrying out my research I was fortunate enough to arrange a series of discussions with Dr. D.W. Winnicott an authority on child psychotherapy. Winnicott described how the bad experiences of life, particularly those of childhood, can remain as it were 'frozen' inside us, leading in severe cases to what is regarded as mental illness[2]. He suggested that for most of us, these undigested disasters are reached and unfrozen by the various phenomena of ordinary life, namely friendships, poetry, music and nursing during physical illness *etc*. He summed it up, and I quote our conversation:

> People who are ill (and we are all ill to some extent) have drive to cure themselves. Nothing is more important than to do that. This means they experience a great need to feel real, and they only come to feel real by doing something like **regression to childhood dependence**, to something which can hold them. This may be realised, for example in the church in or in music.

Since Winnicott extends the idea of illness to cover everybody, he meant that regression to childhood dependence is a feature of normal life.

During these discussions many half formed ideas began to fall into place, and I became aware that I could describe my own experience of having periods of feeling autonomous and self-reliant, and periods when I needed to engage in different activities where I relied on other people and on other resources.

Before I relate the third happening I would like to look more closely at two concepts referred to by Winnicott: **'regression' and 'dependence'**. Both terms refer primarily to states of mind.

---

[2] D W Winnicott **Collected Papers: Through Paediatrics to Psycho-Analysis** London Tavistock (1958) P.284

The key is the way the two concepts are linked together as part of a **developmental process**. One instance comes from a study of children by John Holt[3]. He describes his experience of observing young children with their mothers:
> The courage of little children (and not them alone) rises and falls, like the tide - only for them the cycles are in minutes, or even seconds. We can see this vividly when we watch infants of two or so walking with their mothers, or playing in a playground or par.
> Not along ago I saw this scene in the Public Garden in Boston. The mothers were chatting on a bench while children roamed around. For a while they would explore boldly and freely, ignoring their mothers. Then, after a while, they would use up their store of courage and confidence, and run back to their mothers' sides, and cling there for a while, as if to recharge their batteries. After a moment or two of this they were ready for more exploring, and so they went out, then cam back, and then ventured out again.

He describes his experience of teaching a young child to swim:
> In just the same way, this baby in the pool had his times of exploration, and his times of retreat and retrenchment. At times he let me tow him around freely, kicking his feet and paddling his hands. At other times he gripped my arms fiercely, pulled himself towards me, and by his gestures and expression showed me that he wanted to be held in the same tight and enveloping grip with which we had begun. Or he might even ask to go back to the steps, or to be lifted out of the pool altogether. Then, a few minutes later, he would be back in the water and ready for more adventure.

Holt goes on:
> At one time or another I have watched a number of parents trying to teach their very little children to swim. On the whole, they don't get very far, because they are so insensitive

---

[3] J Holt **How Children Learn** USA: Pitman: Harmondsworth: Penguin (1970) p110

to this rise and fall of courage in the child. Is it because they don't notice? Or because they don't care? Perhaps they feel that the child's feelings are unimportant, to be easily overridden by exhortation and encouragement, or even anger and treats (1970 edition, p.110)

This type of behaviour, has its close counterpart in the images of the relationship between Israel (for the worshipper) and God which we find in, for example, the Psalms.
> But be not far from me, O Lord: thou art my succour, haste thee to help me. (Psalm, 22:19)
> Yea, though I walk through the valley of the shadow of death, I will fear no evil: for thou art with me; thy rod and thy staff comfort me. (Psalm 23:4)

I have used the term '**oscillation**' to refer to the alternation of the periods of autonomous activity and periods of physical or symbolic contact with sources of renewal. For most people, the ordering of everyday life provides for regular cycles of oscillation. Each day includes periods when we address ourselves to the problems of living, and periods when we are fed and cared for, relax, reflect and sleep. Similarly, for many, the week and the year provide occasions for more complete disengagement from the problems of living, in the weekend break and the annual holiday.

I want to draw special attention the words in Winnicott's phrase "**regression** to childhood **dependence**".

Dependence

In using the term 'dependence' to describe a state of mind, I do so to emphasise the natural condition of all living beings - that is they are contingent, wholly reliant upon their interaction with the objects which constitute their environment - air, food, shelter, other human beings etc. I describe it as the state of '**in-needness**'. This 'in-needness' compels me to reach out to others, from the baby seeking the mothers breast, to the astronaut using the power of rockets to fly.

What this in-needness achieves is to bring us into contact with the world around us and into relation with one another as people. This condition is the foundation of all human relations of love, trust, hate, greed, generosity, power - the actual feelings depending upon whether I seek to satisfy my in-needness by working alongside others, or by being in conflict with them. Human society in all its forms, the family, the community, the church, is derived from the commonality of in-needness. I would go so far as to say that our state of human in-needness is not primarily so that we would have food or shelter, but for the development of the relations between the peoples who are necessary for their provision. the in-needness is not satisfied biologically, it has a relational dimension.

In-needness needs to be distinguished from 'having needs'. The former is the given state, the latter is the identification of external things, people, artefacts which at any time I may indicate I "lack", "have need of", or "want". The focus is then on the yearning for the object, the something, or someone not on the origins of the need. This is why getting what one 'needs' never satisfies. It can only gratify for the time being. To argue about what is most important to have need of, is more a matter of culture and race, of class, status, age, health and belief.

Based on this argument about 'in-needness' I define the concept of 'dependence' as a state of mind deriving from 'in-needness' which is not one of helplessness.

An example comes from a study carried out into the personalities of American astronauts.[4]

> Although these men tend to be **individualists** who show a high degree of self-reliance and a clear preference for independent action, all are reported to be **'comfortable when dependence on others is required'** and to have a **'capacity to maintain trust, in what might seem conditions of distrust'**. The performance of the crew of

---

[4] J Bowlby **Attachment and Loss, Vol. 2 Loss** London: Hogarth Press and Institute of Psycho-Analysis (1973) P344

Apollo 13, which met with a mishap en route to the moon, is testimony to their capacity to sustain trust. Not only did they maintain their own efficiency in conditions of great danger but they continued to co-operated trustingly and effectively with their companions at the base on earth.

In other contexts 'dependence' is used to describe enfeeblement and exaggerated reliance on other people, or on specific substances e.g. alcohol, drugs. In these instances I prefer the term 'dependency'. The state of the dependence can lead to many different types of behaviour, **functional behaviour** for the health and development of the individual, group or community; or **dysfunctional behaviour**, leaving the individual, group or community alienated, shut up in their own worlds and unable to develop or grow naturally. The dynamics of the oscillation process is intended to throw light on why on some occasions, dependence leads to development and growth, or to stagnation, retardation and sterility.

Regression

For many writers on human dynamics, regression has such overtones of psychotic, or infantile behaviour, that they have rejected it for alternatives when writing about creative processes (e.g. Bettleheim, Ehrenzweig etc.). But I have retained it with other human scientists (Winnicott, Hartman, Bion and Kris). The antipathy it arouses, is in part a reaction to the process signified, and not just to its misleading associations.

Whether regression is functional or dysfunctional depends upon the circumstances. Here is an example, from a work of fiction in which involuntary regression obscures the capacity of the hero, Paul, to enter into an adult relationship with his boss, Kroner:

> Kroner's enormous, hairy hand closed about Paul's, and Paul, in spite of himself, felt docile, and loving, and childlike. It was as though Paul stood in the enervating, emasculating presence of his father again. Kroner, his father's closest friend, had always made him feel that way, and seemingly wanted **to make him feel** that way. Paul had sworn a

thousand times to keep his wits about him the next time he met Kroner. But it was a matter beyond his control, and at each meeting, as now, the power and resolve were all in the big hands of the older man.[5]

It will be seen that, in this incident, Paul does not cease to be aware that he and Kroner are adults who have a working relationship; he does not in this sense lose touch with reality. Yet his feelings and behaviour are in part dictated by another image of their relationship, according to which Kroner is his father and he is a little boy. His predominant feelings are therefore of being "docile, and loving, and childlike", though somewhere inside himself he feels quite the opposite.

I am using the term 'regression' to describe the mental state experienced which follows a shift from the **outwardly focused** activity and thoughts, characteristic of a planned and regulated life style, to **inwardly unfocused** or chaotic thought and feelings detached from external realities. This transition may or may not be expressed in overt behaviour, so those experiencing regression may not recognise or acknowledge it. When they do they may as it were, 'try and pull themselves together', stop being anxious, overcome stress, and try and pretend to act normally as if nothing had happened. But our hypothesis is that a shift in mental state inevitably occurs, acknowledged or not.

The shift can take many forms. The person may experience anxiety, suddenly being triggered off by their own thoughts. Bad news, misfortune or a death in the family, loss of control due to excessive stress, threats to one's survival, or mental illness, can cut off the person from their immediate surroundings, isolate them and turn them in on themselves. Another form of shift is deliberate withdrawal: taking a holiday, relaxing among friends, a theatre outing, going on retreat or attending a church service, or retiring to bed. In these latter instances the outward behaviour is intended to allow the inner mental shift to take place involuntarily but it may

---

[5] K Vonnegut **Piano Player** London: McMillan (1967) p37

need the stimulus of being cosseted, exhortation, alcohol, or prayer to get it going.

To regress is consciously or unconsciously to search for something or someone on whom to depend. Hence the term to "regress to dependence" is used by Winnicott both as a process which takes place in psychotherapy, and as a feature of normal human growth and development: Frank Lake also used the same idea in his "dynamic cycle of being".

Oscillation

In maintaining that the recurring phases constitute a natural human process, which carried on throughout our lives, I preferred the term 'oscillation' to that of 'cyclic'. The latter has repetitive implications, whereas oscillation suggests that variety and that if we could find ways of plotting the process the amplitude and shape of the curve would alter considerably over time in each phase.

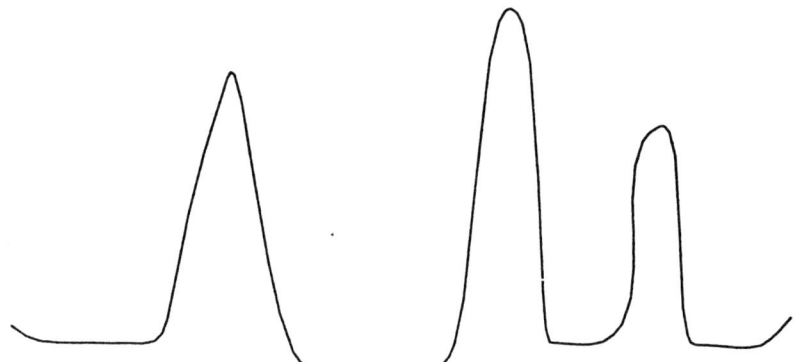

Diagram of the Process of Oscillation

There are too many variables however to conceive the process as scientifically measurable. Oscillation is better conceived as no more than a metaphor about human behaviour - an idea we can play with in our minds.[6]

Systemic Thinking

This discussion leads me into the encounter which opened up for me the third disclosure in developing this theme. In the course of studying organisational behaviour I and some others were joined in the exploration by two Italians, Luigi Boscolo and George Ceechin who, with their colleagues in Milan, had initiated a new mode of family therapy.

They showed that if the family as a whole were willing to be treated as the patient, they were able to consider that the symptoms exhibited by one member e.g. *anorexia nervosa*, was a function of the relation within the family - parents, siblings and extending to grand-parents and other relations. One person could not be given therapy apart from the whole family, as the Milan group conceived that the whole was expressed through its parts, even though the persons involved were unconscious of what was happening. By enabling the family meeting together to entertain this notion, the therapists were able to give paradoxical injunction to different family members to allow them to break across previous habitual repetitive relations. This set up different dynamics in the family system leading to the central person ceasing to display the pathological symptoms. At the behavioural level this method carried further the pioneering work of the Tavistock Institute on groups. It gave substance to **holistic** as distinct from **linear** approaches to behaviour. The major transformation for myself was to discover that I now saw the world differently, I viewed it systematically. As individuals strive to work out their own destinies they are inevitably reflecting and representing others, so that parts and wholes cannot be considered independently. As I mentioned, this theory was already well known to me and applied in my work in the Grubb Institute, but the disclosure resulted

---

[6] J Gleik **Chaos** London Harmondsworth Penguin (1989) p28. Those familiar with the 'Lorenz Attractor' (as James Gleik called it), as a metaphor for exploring chaos may be able to enrich the metaphor

in, to use Thomas Kuhn's term, a new **"paradigm"**, when values, ideas, activities and principles came together in new configurations e.g. **the idea of oscillation as a human process.** It did not happen all at once, but it progressed as I became familiar with the radical changes in the outlook of the so-called new sciences. As Ilya Prigogine and Isabelle Stengers write:

> Both the macroscopic and microscopic levels, the natural sciences have rid themselves of a conception of objective reality that implied that novelty and diversity had to be denied in the name of immutable universal laws. They have rid themselves of a fascination with a rationality taken as closed, and a knowledge seen as nearly achieved. They are now open to the unexpected, which they no longer define as the result of imperfect knowledge or insufficient control.[7]

A WORKING HYPOTHESIS

I turn now to the working hypothesis I want to explore in this paper **the oscillation theory provides a metaphor of life as a psycho-dynamic process which indicates essential conditions for the well-being of society from a Christian perspective.**

I have identified four stages or modes in the oscillation process. I have given each stage a distinctive name to symbolise the successive changes in the conscious or unconscious state of mind without restricting the range of experience they attempt to describe as they merge into and replace one another.

Realisation

If I followed Wincing closely I would call the stage - "independence", in contra-distinction to dependence. However 'independence' only hints at one aspect of life in this stage - that of feeling free to take one's own decisions. Since a fuller description is to say the person is trying to express what they consider themselves

---

[7] I Prigogine and I Stengers **Order out of Chaos** London: Fontana (1985)

to be or becoming I call it **Realisation.** Realisation is the actual outward behaviour expressing the person's inward being in a context. A context where persons relate with one another to achieve things and satisfy their in-needness. Creative thought is being realised in: an invention, a picture, an opera, a poem, a home, a supermarket, running a business, pastoring a congregation and planning a war - the innovations being reflected in and through others and manifest in artefacts and their use.

Regression to Dependence
For this mode, I use the term **Regression to Dependence** to symbolise the inward withdrawal by a person from engagement in their habitual round of activities, and the withdrawal of their own ego-strength from working with others. As I have mentioned earlier, 'regression' as a term is frequently used by other human scientists.

Identification
This stage is called **Identification** in order to symbolise the search for a dependent object or person with whom to identify, to be a container for their anxiety which has been aroused by regression. Identification is extremely complex and varied where people are searching for help in finding out who they are, who they **really** are. To use Winnicott's phrase, they want to "feel real". This stage in the oscillation is where the parts, fragmented in regression are brought together, at deep levels of conscious or unconscious thought or dreams. They contribute to the creative work of the self and the community, or a work of art or scientific discovery which is realised at a latter stage. This is the stage of culture formation where community members evolve rituals to create tribal identification, exemplified for example in the primitive ritual behaviour on the terraces of football stadia.

Transformation to Realisation
Transformation is the stage of transition between identification the realisation stages. Like the caterpillar which emerges from the

cocoon as a butterfly, the newly re-constructed ego is being transformed so that it can express outwardly, the inward process of creativity. The process is one of transformation which gradually merges into the stage of realisation.

Oscillation Process in Context
By this time it is obvious to you that this broad outline of human life is not new. Myths and legends of many ages and cultures have pictured the dying and rising of the gods, the ritual death before the new birth into full tribal membership. Scholars in the fields of anthropology, sociology, political philosophy and psychology have arrived at descriptions of social life and mentality which reflect a binary form of human existence, referred to by Emile Durkheim as *homo duplex*. Victor Turner an anthropologist concluded that 'society seems to be a process rather than a thing - dialectical process with successive modalities of '*structure*' (organised existence), and '*communitas*' (where restraints are relaxed). Human scientists have explored the behaviour and experience of those moving from one modality to the other, from the perspective of psych-analysis, and also those analysing how artforms are created. This paper is not the place to make a detailed comparison with other theories of this rhythm of life and death. But one or two observations are in order.

We have pointed out that the state of in-needness has brought about the formation of communities and societies, but it is the myths of those communities, frequently associated with the repetitious patterns of the movements of the heavenly bodies, the tides and the seasons, seed-time and harvest, which have affected the quality and the culture of the lives and development of these communities. The stories, amalgams of fantasy and fact, have until recently been underestimated by the so-called advanced civilised peoples, convinced of the validity of universal objective truths. But in the light of the subjective dimension of truth being disclosed through the new sciences and philosophies, these stories are being reassessed, and we are becoming more humble towards primitive or ancient peoples of past civilisations.

The assumption many of us were reared with, was that of a progression from simple to complex, from ignorance to truth, from superstition to faith. Our lives were planned and we were educated and preached to, on this general model of progress. This was the model which treated these ancient myths as irrelevant to understanding life today, our lives. What the oscillation process may do is to enable people to question those earlier assumptions as they re-examine their own experience carefully. We are not as secure in our knowledge as we imagined we were a few years ago, and we need new tools of interpretation of our existence.

A second observation is about the pattern underlying the chaos. However bewildered we are, it is a safe assumption that the earth will continue rotating so the sun will continue to appear to rise and set daily, the moon will wax and wane, the tides rise and fall, the seasons come and go. It is these natural phenomena which provide rhythms for the oscillation processes. The timing of the recurrent stages as we normally experience them are normally measured, but no determined, for us by the calendar, into days, months and years. Though this pattern is continually disturbed by sudden changes in our lives it reminds us in planning to satisfy our in-needness of how much we take for granted. It is interesting to note that the resource the human race has probably most taken as free and always available - air to breathe, is now being threatened.

ANALYSIS OF THE OSCILLATION PROCESS
In the second and final part of this paper I want to pen up the oscillation process to discover and display more plainly our relationship with God.
A Jewish Perspective
This brings me to a follow-up story to that of the Rabbi who spoke only of life, not of religion. Time allows only for a sketchy outline of a multi-faith project carried out some years ago in Birmingham, as a means of providing support to different faiths as they each tried to explore how their own faith enabled them to carry out a major responsibility they agreed they had in common with other faith groups - that of being citizens of Birmingham. There were 15 different groups including Anglicans, Church of Christ, Roman Catholics, Methodist, German Lutherans, Black Pentecostal, United Reformed Church, Chinese Christians, Jews, Buddhists, Sikhs, Muslims, and Hindus. Over the two years of the project, members working separately in their own homogenous faith groups discussed a basic question about living in Birmingham, then sent representatives to a meeting to share their finds, there they agreed on the next step, and decided on another question for group discussion. During the project, all the discussions and reports were recorded and circulated among the groups. In the process of working with papers of the group meetings, I cam across something unexpected. While groups had different approaches, they all had certain basic similarities with the exception of one group - the Jews. While the other faith groups spoke from a religious perspective, the Jews constantly addressed the issue from a human point of view. When I pointed this out at the meeting of representatives I was not popular with the two Jewish representatives present. Many months had to pass before they began to see that I had been speaking positively about their approach. They had believed I was denying they were expressing their faith; what I found difficulty in communicating to them was that what impressed me, was their capacity to **express their faith by the**

way they spoke of their life as citizens. Only then did I recall what the Rabbi had said.

I recognise I may have tantalised you, by only giving an outline of what was to me a profound experience. Over those months in the project I grasped that these Jews in expressing who they were as human beings in the world, were stating who they were in relation to God in a wholly integrated way. In the terms of the oscillation process, they **were realising themselves**. It gave me a new insight into the way the gospels were written about Jesus, why he spoke of the Kingdom of God and very little about the Church. Professor Walter Brueggemann, the Old Testament scholar, in his lectures on *The Bible and Post-Modern Imagination*[8] has insisted that today we Christians are called to behave like Jews, if we are to imagine how we need to live in the current world situation.

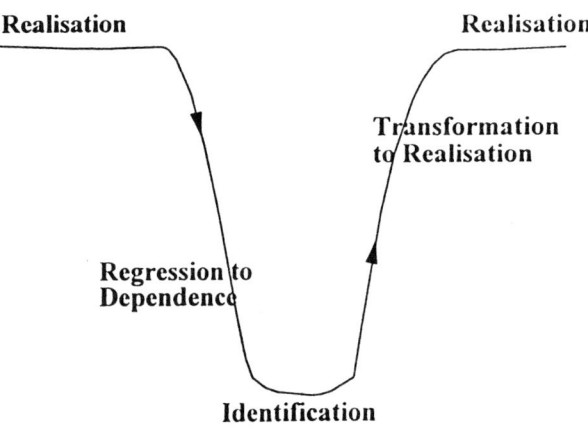

One Phase of Oscillation diagram

REALISATION MODE

In the **Realisation** mode, how I behave shows who I am, and what goes on in a community **is** that community, it exists no-where else. In this mode, the indicative mood prevails, not the 'oughts', 'should' or 'must' of the subjunctive. This is where the inner world of the

---

[8] W Brueggeman **The Bible and Post-Modern Imagination** London: SCM (1993)

person group or community is made manifest. It is the art gallery of the works we have been making and inventing and contriving within ourselves - the truth of what we **are**, is being displayed. I am not making any moral or ethical judgement. That there may not be those who can understand or interpret my behaviour to me or to themselves does not alter the facts. The family, the business, the laboratory, the sports field, the benefit office, the streets, are where we are expressing ourselves in reality. We may be understood, we may be making mistakes, or we may be trying to hide something, even from ourselves. This is our life.

Within the systemic framework I mentioned earlier, this behaviour can be given meaning in relating to that of others which at first sight is quite separate, *e.g.* much of my own professional work in analysing organisations addresses this issue. For example why does a Sales Director behave incompetently?

That seems an easy question. But after this one is fired, what does it mean when his successor, and next successor exhibit the same incompetence? Finally it dawns on the Chief Executive the problem is that he himself is behaving as the Sales Director, and he allows them to fail because he did not want to change his own way of working. By thinking systemically, when anything appears to be wrong, we ask "Why does the situation need this to happen?" Paradoxical though it may appear, such an approach can unravel complicated predicaments if we persist questioning.

It is in this mode that great things are achieved. The creative outworkings of our finest thoughts are presented in our culture, in our politics, and in our environment, and provide the resources by which we live and work together. These developments however are threatened by feelings of destructiveness spawned by conflicting thoughts and attitudes about the acquisition of resources to satisfy needs, leading to destructive competition. We all partake of the beauty and excellence in some measure; but likewise generate the darkness which destroys.

Realisation, was I have said, is the outworking of the prior modes of the oscillation. Behaviour if it is to change positively requires that we take steps to allow it alter and adapt as we experience and engage in the other modes. For the Christian this realisation mode is where the Kingdom of God comes.

God's Invisibility

George Goyder, an old friend, used to tease people by asking "Why is God invisible?" then to supply the response: "Because all good servants in a household are 'invisible' in the way they go about their work". Jesus' parable in St. Matthew's gospel about the Last Judgement, where the king separates the sheep from the goats throws light on this. The sheep were welcomed because they were those, who without realising it, in satisfying the hungry, the thirsty, the strangers, the naked, the sick and the prisoners, were serving the King himself.

> "Truly I say to you, as you did it to one of the least of these my brothers, you did it to me". (Matt.25)

It was the goats who were rejected. They neglected the King, because they saw only human weakness and poverty and did nothing about it.

The parable shows two things are hidden in this life: the presence of the King among the needy and the oppressed, and the membership of the Kingdom of God. The sheep are expressing their membership, without knowing it. The invisibility of the King is to ensure that the motive for serving in the name of the King, is the in-needness of humanity. It is to respond to human in-needness as human need not because Jesus tells them to, by engaging with the political and social issues of society naturally, as citizens. It is this kind of thing the Jewish group were saying in the multi-faith project.

This argument finds support in the saying of Jesus (using Eugene Petersen's graphic translation)

> The kingdom of God doesn't come by counting the days on the calendar. Nor when someone says - look here, or there it is! And why? Because God's kingdom is ready among you (Luke 7:20)

Underneath this outward expression there is inward experience. The reliability of disciplined behaviour frequently results from the resolution of a struggle with anxiety; the decisive action after taking risks generated through facing uncertainty, and the calm approach belying turbulent and chaotic feelings. Just as a violin needs a taut string to sing the pure notes, so human beings need to work with stress as a condition for staying alive. As Von Bertalanffy writes

> Biologically, life is not maintenance or restoration of **equilibrium** but is essentially maintenance of **disequilibrium**, as the doctrine of the organism as an open system reveals. Reaching equilibrium means death and decay. Psychologically, behaviour not only tends to release tensions but also builds up tensions: if this stops, the patient is a decaying mental corpse in the same way a living organism becomes a body in decay when tensions and forces keeping it from equilibrium have stopped.[9]

The building up of tensions and their release is a process linked with creativity. The creative act issues from the building up; the act of creation releases the tension for the time being. To allow ourselves to be subjected to stress in relation to our environment can therefore be a positive condition for the transformation of that environment.

REGRESSION MODE

But there is not suggestion that this is a linear process. Just as John Holt describes the children running back to their mothers for support when their fear overcomes them, so the tensions build up in us and we look for ways of coping - we enter into the mode of Regression. The situation may be one in which the individual feels he no longer has the resources to meet its challenge, either because of the magnitude of the task or through the depletion of his own resources or one which in the past has usually be within his competence. In extreme cases he may be on the verge of collapsing.

---

[9] L von Bertalanffy **General System Theory** Harmondsworth Penguin Edition (1967) p191

Opportunities for regression may also be sought by the individual, consciously or intuitively, in order to find freedom to re-enter and re-examine past experience, particularly the bad experiences which, in Winnicotts's terms, have been 'frozen', because they were at the time too bad to be contemplated.

On other occasions the response occurs at predetermined times and places. Just as Pavlov's dogs looked for food when they heard a bell rung, so the thoughts of some churchgoers turn to God when they hear church bells! As we shall discuss further later, the individual's rhythm of oscillation is partially synchronised with that of others in any group or community.

Whatever the reason, the actual regression process may take various forms, and may turn out to be creative or destructive, or merely to maintain the status quo in the life of the individual. Kris (1952)[10] and Winnicott (1965)[11] use the expression 'regression in the service of the ego' to distinguish creative regression from the less organised process in which the ego is overwhelmed by regression.

Creative regression to dependence

Creative regression to dependence requires a suitable setting, a **'facilitating environment'**. In psychotherapy this is provided by the physical setting, and by the attention, understanding and security conveyed by the therapist. In worship also it is conveyed by the surroundings, and by the quality of attention conveyed by those who lead it. In these and other situations, however, creative regression is only possible if the individual, or group of individuals, is **able and will to use** the conditions provided. It is necessary for the individual to be able, in the present situation, to 'cash in' on the experiences of good-enough mothering which he has received in the past. He requires memories of dependence, in order to be able to take the risk, and tolerate the anxieties of, dependence. This is perhaps a psychological version of the statement in the Letter to the Hebrews,

---

[10] E Kris **Psychoanalytic Explorations in Art** New York: Schoken Books (1964)

[11] D W Winnicott **The Maturational Process and the Facilitating Environment** London: Hogart Press and Institute of Psycho-Analysis (1965)

that 'anyone who comes to God must believe that he exists and that he rewards those who search for him' (11:6)

Creative regression to dependence thus entails a conscious act on the part of the individual, of placing himself in the hands of another, with due appreciation of the risks involved, but with some hope,. It is not a means of escape from stress or danger, but a means of re-entering the disaster area under conditions in which there is freedom not to be defensive. In therapy, the patient's awareness of risk indicates that she remains in contact with everyday reality, however tenuously, throughout the process of regression and reintegration. However alarming and potentially overwhelming the emotional world into which she enters, she retains somewhere in her mind the knowledge of what she is up to and where she is. Winnicott refers to this unregressed element in the personality as the 'observing ego', which remains identified with the therapist.[12]

The promise of creative regression to dependence is, in the psychotherapy of Winnicott, Balint, and Kahn, a new beginning in which the patient is able to let go of the habitual ways of seeing the world and herself, which in the past have constituted her bondage, and to begin to find/construct a new world and a new self, and correspondingly new patterns of behaviour.

Defensive regression to dependence

In psycho-analysis it has been shown that under certain conditions patients enter upon a form of regression to a primitive state, in which they make increasing demands for attention and gratification which can never be satisfied. The patient reaches an addiction-like state in which he is terrified of the withdrawal of the care he is receiving. He has no observing ego who sees the regression as a search for a new beginning and an enhanced life. Whereas in creative regression the patient is aware that he and the therapist are engaged in a co-operative venture, defensive regression leads to temporary states in which the patient feels relieved of all anxiety and the therapist is

---

[12] D W Winnicott (1958) p289

taken for granted. This sense of security is highly precarious. Because he has totally handed over responsibility for his welfare to someone else, the patient is thrown into a panic when it appears that the therapist is not providing safety. When someone deliberately enters a lift in order to descend to the ground floor he is not thrown into a panic when the lift begins to move downwards; but if he feels the floor of his living room begins to give way under his feet he is thrown into a panic, because the dependability of the floor is something he has taken for granted.

Defensive regression is an impossible attempt to return to the innocence of infancy. By contrast, creative regression does not nurse the illusion that there can be a return to the cradle or the womb. This is why recovery from creative regression is frequently accompanied by anger and mourning, since with his renewed vision the patient recognises more clearly the years and their possibilities which have been wasted in partial living. This mourning is expressed by St. Augustine in his Confessions:

> Too late came I to love thee, O thou Beauty both so ancient and so fresh, yea too late came I to love thee. And behold, thou wert within me, and I out of myself, when I make search for thee.[13]

Therapists also refer to what seems to be a distinct form of defensive regression, when on occasions patients have withdrawn briefly into a waking sleep or reverie; they have 'switched off'.

John Updike (1968) provides a fictional example in a church service of this:

> On command, Piet sat and prayed. Prayer was an unsteady state of mind for him. When it worked, he seemed, for intermittent moments, to be in the farthest corner of a deep burrow, a small endearing hairy animal curled up as if to hibernate. In this condition he felt close to a massive warm

---

[13] Augustine **Confessions** London (Everyman Edition) 1907

secret, like the heart of lava at the earth's core. His existence for a second seemed to evade decay.[14]

Fragmentation and Projection

Outwardly regression may appear controlled where there is an expectation of a dependable object, but whether controlled or uncontrolled, the person experiences an inner fragmentation of themselves into good and bad parts. In her work, Melanie Klein concluded that in the infant/mother relationship the child's behaviour was affected by fantasies which alternate between two positions - what she called the *paranoid-schizoid*, and the *depressive* positions.[15] In the paranoid-schizoid position extensive splitting occurs and the child projects the good parts and bad parts of himself into the mother who is imagined to be two different persons - for example the 'good' breast and the 'bad' breast.

In regression the person conceives of others on which to project those fragmented parts of themselves. Hence the evolution of myths about God and the devil, which has been commented upon by philosophers like Feuerback, Neitzsche, and also by Freud. The idea is as old as the Greeks, and also attributed to animals by Xenophanes.

> Now if horses or oxen or lions had hands to paint and make works of art that men make, then would horses give their gods horse-like forms in painting or sculpture, and oxen oxen-like forms, even each after its own kind.[16]

The search for a dependable object or person, whether a myth or reality, is critical to health and well-being - for salvation. The merit of the writers of the Psalms is that they experience Yahweh as one who could receive all their projections, good and bad. This represents the profound understanding of these writers which Walter

---

[14] J Updike **Couples** London: Andre Deutsch (1968)

[15] M Klein **The Writings of Melanie Klein** London: Hogarth (1975) Vol 3 P48-56

[16] Xenophones 6th Century BC, quoted by Clement of Alexandria **Stromateis**, 5.109.2

Brueggemann shows when he classifies most of the psalms under the headings of "Orientation, Dis-orientation and Re-orientation".[17] In those of 'Dis-orientation' he points out that the psalmist can express both his own despair about himself and his despair and anger towards a caring Yahweh and relate them together.

In addition to despair, there is also the sense of failure and of guilt - no wonder the gods are feared even when they are longed for. As the writer to the Hebrews says:

"It is a fearful thing to fall into the hands of the living God"

And again speaking of the need to worship God in the way he finds acceptable, in reverence and fear, he says:

"For our God is a consuming fire."

With this quotation we move from Regression to the stage of Identification.

IDENTIFICATION MODE

This is the mode of myths, legends, dreams, symbols visions, and revelations. A sphere of dying and rising, death and resurrection and of the creative imagination. Tribes and peoples since time in memorial have experienced a special quality in this experience which they have called 'sacred' and devised rituals and liturgies with which to steer them through its mysteries which is illustrated by great art and profound music. For example Mozart takes the fragmented and ambiguous stories that comprise *The Magic Flute* and transforms them so that we can get in touch with the menace and liberation of human existence.

I have no wish to enter into a discussion of the merits of these different systems in providing environments which seek to enable people to feel real. What I will do is to take the example of Christian worship, which I have studied over the years and also because it is something which comes from my own experience. Since dependence is the state of mind underlying the identification stage it implies we

---

[17] W Brueggemann **The Message of the Psalms** Minneapolis: Augsburg (1984) p19

have **faith** in who or whatever we regress to. Worshipping God within the body of a congregation is one way of searching which I now wish to explore.

Worship in Church
Church buildings are usually larger than needed in comparison with the human scale. They invite us to imagine something greater than ourselves and open us to see beyond the immediate *here and now*. Stained glass, sculpture, vivid colours, and memorials underline this sense of awe. Entering such a building becomes a preparation for worship, providing a facilitating environment. Karl Barth gives an outsider's impression of this

> Everyone must apparently, perhaps without wishing it, speak of God. And then the minister will have the congregation sing ancient songs full of weird and weighty memories, strange ghostly witnesses of the sufferings, struggles, and triumphs of the long-departed fathers, all leading to the edge of an immeasurable event, all, whether the minister and people understand what they are singing or not, full of reminiscences of God, always of God. 'God is present! God *is* present.'[18]

Familiarity has perhaps numbed our feelings of mystery and awe, reawakened when we visit a strange cathedral, but habitually leaving us taking our surroundings in church for granted. The more comfortable and easy it becomes, the more our regression tends to be defensive: Because we have avoided the depths of dying, we can not scale the height of new life. Alternatively we can treat the place as unchanging as if God were dead, and changes in liturgy or furnishings arouse hostility or grief, indicating our own fragility. We want to go out from church without ourselves changing or developing, like Piet in John Updike's story.

The point I am making is that well designed churches are built to facilitate our creative regression to dependence. The act of private

---

[18] K Barth **The Word, God and the Word of Man** London: Hodder & Stoughton (1928)

prayer when going to our seat is a positive response to this. Jesus' words 'Except you become as little children you will not enter the Kingdom of Heaven', is a warning to those who wish to attend church as if they were listening to a university lecture.
We are invited to surrender our creative minds, to face the uncertainty of what we are doing. No wonder we need to trust God!

The Church Service - Liturgy
Then the liturgy is spread before us; to allow us to participate at the psychic level for which our regression has prepared us. the confession may be either an occasion for telling ourselves we could do better, or for accepting the pain of guilt, speaking of our helplessness and our accountability for our sins to God, who can contain all the damage we have done to others. When the minister pronounces forgiveness, it is god offering it to us on behalf of all those we have offended, many of whom we don't know, and because we cannot be sure of the effects of what we have done. Here the boundaries between God and ourselves and between each other are dissolved. We become one with each other in our reconciliation. What Freud called the "oceanic feeling of religious experience" may follow, stimulated by hymns, music, and dance, offering our praise and thanks to God. People who have not hitherto been in touch with the depth of their emotions may spontaneously engage in strange and manic behaviour. Whether this is the working of God the Holy Spirit depends upon the outcomes - does it produce the fruits of the Spirit as Paul says: love, joy, peace, gentleness and so on? Sadly, in some churches the shaking of the hands to signify the sharing of the peace, instead of promoting identification of one with another, reduces the sense of wholeness and oneness by the individual physical encounters, where one sometimes feels left out.
The liturgy seeks to encourage us to use our imagination, not least as we hear the Bible. The stories can evoke ideas and feelings to fill our minds with God. This God who has worked in countless ways with different peoples of every age, **this** is the God we are being called to worship, to be at one with, so that as we identify with Him,

we discover our own identity. Here the sermon, the address can prophesy and give us new visions or talk us into locking up ourselves into dreams of the past. As my father-in-law, an Archdeacon used to say: "However poor the preacher is in his preaching, I can always meditate upon the text."

But there is more. Where the process of identification has extended through the congregation, the prayers for the church and world make more sense. It becomes a representative activity, are example of the whole human system of life and death in operation. The ones who lead the prayers are at the same time addressing God on behalf of the whole, of which they are speaking part, and also asking God to work with those prayed for as being other parts of the same whole. There may be no obvious **relationship** between all these people, but as part of the same system there is a universal **relatedness** which also includes God.

But the Church also has another major resource for this mode, the sacraments of Baptism and Holy Communion each of which has two major symbolic movements - dying and rising, and identification.

In **Baptism** the candidate in passing figuratively through the waters, dies and rises again - the death is to sin, the residue of regression; the rising again is to new life. The identification is with Christ, in his dying in baptism where he himself identified with our sins and his coming out of the waters to proclaim his Kingdom of new life under God. After the baptism identification is then extended to the baptised who have now become incorporated into Christ's body, becoming members one of another in his Church, and inheritors of his Kingdom.

Likewise in **Holy Communion** the celebration is of the death of Christ and his resurrection, where, as we eat bread and drink wine we are made one with him, both in his dying and in his rising again. Here the incorporation is physically symbolised by the eating and drinking. The God on whom we projected, has received not only our good parts, but accepted our bad parts and reconciled them, in Christ. Our fragmented parts are made whole as he is in us, and we in him.

The great accomplishment of the Christian Church is that it has developed a liturgy over the centuries which enables human beings to work through the stage of identification, in discovering a meaning for life.

Becoming whole persons
The consequence of this new life is to become *perfect* in the St. Paul's sense, *i.e.* to be made fit for God's use in the world. Now, there is no need for us to project unimagined parts of ourselves on others, *i.e.* to blame them, or to become *satans* to them *i.e.* accusers. Nor, is it to be envious of others. We who are experiencing reconciliation with God in Christ are now able to reconcile within our own selves both good and bad parts, in technical terms, to re-introject them, and to integrate them to become whole persons. Referring back to Melanie Klein's two positions deriving from the relation between child and mother, but here applied to the relation between us humans and the Creator; it can be said that the members of the Church in their identification mode, have moved from the *paranoid-schizoid* position referred in the regression stage, to the second *depressive* position. Klein calls it **depressive** because the individual is well aware of past behaviour with its hurt to others, and seeks to make reparation for it, by the way he/she lives in the future. Klein regards this as the foundation of all creative work, even though it may only be felt unconsciously .
When the person fails to re-introject the bad parts, but only the good, then there is mania. There are Christians like this who consider their redemptions means that their sins and their consequences have been completely blotted out so that they become sinless. Where they believe this, manic behaviour is likely to follow, which can be mistaken for the next stage in oscillation.

TRANSFORMATION MODE
The process has now reached the fourth stage, that of **Transformation to Realisation**.

It is vital to recognise that in the Identification mode, all is **symbolic**. However there is need of psychic space to learn how to express the symbols to become **real** in life, in our actual behaviour *i.e.* the realisation mode.

Why then do I propose this Transformation mode, why cannot Identification immediately lead to Realisation?

Transformation is the stage where the re-constituted person hangs out 'L' plates, preferably green ones! It provides a space for the rich symbols of the previous stage to work to the surface, in particular to become aware of the systemic dimension of the context which might have unfamiliar features, certainly different from those seen symbolically.

There are those who confuse the symbols with the real and wish to conduct their lives as if the Identification stage was the only one, or the most important. It is to them that Samuel Greg addresses the hymn, picturing them as the three apostles on the mountain after Jesus was transfigured before them.

> Stay, Master, stay upon this heavenly hill;
> A little longer, let us linger still;
> With all the mighty ones of old beside,
> Near to the aweful Presence still abide;
> Before the throne of light we trembling stand,
> And catch a glimpse into the spirit-land.
> No, saith the Lord, the hour is past, we go;
> Our home, our life, our duties lie below.
> While here we kneel upon the mount of prayer,
> The plough lies waiting in the furrow there.
> Here we sought God that we might know his will;
> There we must do it, serve him, seek him still.[19]

Without being contentious I suggest that those who confuse the Church with God's Kingdom are in a similar position to the apostles. They try to build up the Church as an organisation to change the world instead of seeing it as the symbol of the Kingdom, where God

---

[19] S Greg (1804-76) **Hymns and Psalms** London Epworth No. 158

rules in love, forgiveness, justice, goodness, peace and hope, through its members working in the world. Jesus taught us to pray "Thy Kingdom come" not "Thy Church come". It is to make the Kingdom real that we are called.

Bearing in mind that the whole oscillation process is a metaphor for human life, in practice all stages overlap and there is no ideal process to discover. People experiencing one stage, are in systemic terms doing it on behalf of those experiencing the other stages. Even though a close knit community might be fairly homogeneous and nominally have the same rhythm and pattern of life-style, the stages of oscillation cannot be read off from what they do together - *e.g.* where everyone goes to church on Sunday it may be for some, no different from going to a social event.

I speak of disciplined activity in engaging and re-engaging with others for the enhancement of life in dealing with in-needness. The transformation is from symbolic activity to **work activity** and this requires psychic adjustment as the unconscious shifts into the depressive position.

The drive which emanates from identification arouses awareness of **power,** power to achieve. Christianly speaking this is explainable as the internal working of the **Holy Spirit** - people with the power of the Spirit. Disconnected from the realities of human tasks pretensions by people to have such power is as dangerous as a loose canon. What impressed the contemporaries of Jesus was his **authority** - he made things happen in accordance with, as he said, his Father's will. It is not for our benefit that we receive the Spirit of power, but to use it with authority in expressing for love for others. This is what we are ultimately accountable for, as human beings defined by our state of in-needness: of God, others, nature and the world.

TO SUM UP
I have now sketched in one cycle of the oscillation process. As I have indicated the process cannot be planned in advance, it is a **dynamic response** to the interaction of the experiences of the outer with our inner world. As individuals work through it for themselves, however alienated they feel, they are functioning as part of a wider system, - remember the flapping of the butterfly wings in the story of the Chaos theory.

I started out with a working hypothesis, and hope that I have provided evidence for you to test it for yourself.

Oscillation is a recurring process throughout life. Much of it is unconscious and its outcomes may not be recognised except over a long period of time. A little here, and a little there, may be the story of the more healthy-than-ill person, but so long as we retain the will to live, according to **my hypothesis** the process will continue; and according to **my faith** God is present with us, Emmanuel, at every stage in every mode and state of mind.

Awareness of these issues can provide the context for us to foster the well-being of society from where we can practice it.

Jesus the Psychologist: exploring the story of two brothers

The Revd Professor Leslie J. Francis

Overview
The parables of Jesus have long been recognised as revealing deep and penetrating insight into human behaviour. The aim of the present chapter is to take *one* personality theory and to set this personality theory to work in exploring *one* of Jesus' best known parables. In this way scripture may be used to test the adequacy of personality psychology, while personality psychology may be used to stimulate insight into scripture.
The personality theory adopted in this chapter is based on Myers Briggs Type Indicator. The parable explored in this chapter comes from Luke's gospel and concerns the less than harmonious relationship between two brothers, their father and the ill-fated fatted calf. It will be argued that the two brothers exemplify very different personality types which generate quite understandable conflict.
There are two main parts to this chapter and each part is crafted in its own distinctive voice. The first part of the chapter provides a succinct overview of the Myers Briggs Type Indicator and a review of the main criticisms to which this theory and instrument are vulnerable. Here the voice is that of the research psychologist. the second part of the chapter discusses the personality profile of the two brothers and interweaves the themes of scripture and psychology. Here the voice is that of the pastoral theologian and preacher. These two parts are separated by the opportunity to hear the uninterpreted voice of scripture.

Personality types
Individuals differ in a number of ways. Not surprisingly, there is no clear common agreement in psychology as to how these differences

between people can be most adequately and economically described, nor as to which differences are essential to the description of personality.

Personality theories themselves may be classified in a number of different ways. One crucial distinction is between those personality theories which have their roots in a theoretical model of human behaviour and those which have their roots in a mathematical model of how observed individual differences cluster. The Myers Briggs Type Indicator belongs to the first of these approaches, with its roots firmly in a theoretical model first proposed by Carl G. Jung.

Carl Jung suggested that individuals differ in two crucial *processes*. The first process concerns the ways in which we gather information. This is the *perceiving* process. Some people prefer *sensing* (S); others prefer *intuition* (N). According to the theory, these two types look at the world in very different ways.

The second process concerns the ways in which we make decisions. This is the *judging* process. Some people prefer *thinking* (T); others prefer *feeling* (F). According to the theory, these two types come to decisions about the world in very different ways.

Jung also suggested that individuals differ in the *orientation* in which they prefer to employ these two processes. Some people prefer the outer or extraverting world (E); others the inner or introverting world (I). According to the theory, these two types are energised in very different ways. Extroverts draw their energy from the outer world of people and things, while introverts draw their energy from their inner world.

Finally, individuals differ in their *attitude* to the outer world. Both introverts and extroverts need to deal with the outer world and both may prefer to do this with a *judging* (J) or a *perceiving* (P) process. According to the theory, these two types display a very different attitude to the outer world.

The Myers Briggs Type Indicator is a multiple-choice questionnaire designed by Katherine C. Briggs and Isabel Briggs-Myers to identify the individual's preferences between introversion and extroversion, between sensing and intuition, between thinking and feeling, and between judging and perceiving. These identified preferences are then expressed in terms of the four preferred letters. The present author's type, for example, is expressed as *INTJ*, indicating preferences for introversion, intuition, thinking and relating to the outer world with a judging process. These preferences doubtlessly emerge in the way in which this chapter has been structured and written.

What the theory understands by these preferences now needs to be explained in greater detail.

Introversion and extroversion

Introversion and extroversion describe the two preferred orientations of the inner world and the outer world. Introverts prefer to focus their attention on the inner world of ideas and draw their energy from that inner world. When introverts are tired and need energising they look to the inner world. Extroverts prefer to focus their attention on the outer world of people and things and draw their energy from that outer world. When extroverts are tired and need energising they look to the outer world.

Introverts like quiet for concentration. They can shut off the distractions of the outer world and turn inwards. They often experience trouble in remembering names and faces. They can work at one solitary project for a long time without interruption. When they are engaged in a task in the outer world they may become absorbed in the ideas behind that task.

Introverts work best along and may resent distractions and interruptions from other people. Introverts dislike being interrupted by the telephone. Introverts think things through before acting and may spend so long in thought that they miss the opportunity to act. Introverts prefer to learn by reading rather than talking with others. They may also prefer to communicate with others in writing, rather than face to face or over the phone. This is particularly the case if they have something unpleasant to communicate.

Introverts are orientated to the inner world. they focus on ideas, concepts and inner understanding. They are reflective. They consider deeply before acting. They probe inwardly for stimulation. Extroverts like variety and action. They can shut off the distractions of the inner world and turn outward. They are good at remembering faces and names and enjoy meeting people and introducing people. They can become impatient with long, slow jobs. When they are working in the company of other people they may become more interested in how others are doing the job than in the job itself. Extroverts like to have other people around them in the working environment. They enjoy the stimulus of sudden interruption and telephone calls. Extroverts like to act quickly and to be decisive, even when it is not totally appropriate to do so.

Extroverts prefer to learn a task by talking it through with other people. They prefer to communicate with other people face to face or over the phone, rather than in writing. They often find that their own ideas become clarified through communicating them with others.

Extroverts are oriented to the outer world. They focus on people and things. They prefer to learn by trial and error and they do so with confidence. They are active people. They scan the outer environment for stimulation.

Sensing and intuition

Sensing and intuition describe the two preferences associated with the *perceiving process*. They describe different preferences used to acquire information. Sensing types focus on the realities of a situation as perceived by the senses. Intuitive types focus on the possibilities, meanings and relationships, the 'big picture' that goes beyond sensory information.

Individuals with a preference for intuition develop insight into complexity. They have the ability to see abstract, symbolic and theoretical relationships, and the capacity to see future possibilities. They put their reliance on inspiration rather than on past experience.

Their interest is in the new and untried. They trust their intuitive grasp of meanings in relationships.

Intuitive types are aware of new challenges and possibilities. They see quickly beyond the information they have been given or the materials they have to hand to the possibilities and challenges which these offer. They are often discontent with the way things are and wish to improve them. They bore quickly and dislike doing the same thing repeatedly.

Individuals with a preference for intuition enjoy learning new skills. They work in bursts of energy, powered by enthusiasm, and then enjoy slack periods between activity.

Intuitive types follow their inspirations and hunches. They may lead to conclusions too quickly and misconstrue the information or get the facts wrong. They dislike taking too much time to secure precision.

Intuitive types may tend to imagine that things are more complex than they really are. They tend to over-complexify things. They are curious about why things are the way they are and may prefer to raise questions than to find answers.

Intuitive types are always striving to gain an overview of the information around them. In terms of an old proverb, they may prefer to pay attention to the two birds in the bush rather than the one in the hand.

Intuitive types perceive with memory and associations. They see patterns and meanings and assess possibilities. They are good at reading between the lines and projecting possibilities for the future. They prefer to go always for the big picture. They prefer to let the mind inform the eyes.

Individuals who have a preference for sensing develop keen awareness of present experience. They have acute powers of observation, good memory for facts and details, the capacity for realism, and the ability to see the world as it is. They rely on experience rather than theory. They put their trust in what is known and in the conventional.

Individuals with a preference for sensing are aware of the uniqueness of each individual event. They develop good techniques of observation and they recognise the practical way in which things work now.

Sensing types like to develop an established way of doing things and gain enjoyment from exercising skills which they have already learnt. Repetitive work does not bore them. They are able to work steadily with a realistic idea of how long a task will take.

Sensing types usually reach their conclusion step by step, observing each piece of information carefully. They are not easily inspired to interpret the information in front of them and they may not trust inspiration when it comes. They are very careful about getting the facts right and are good at engaging in precise work.

Sensing types may fail to recognise complexity in some situations, and consequently over simplify tasks. They are good at accepting the current reality as the given situation in which to work. They would much rather work with the present information than to speculate about future possibilities. They clearly agree with the old proverb that the bird in the hand is worth two in the bush.

Sensing types perceive clearly with the five senses. They attend to practical and factual details. They are in touch with physical realities. They attend to the present moment and prefer to confine their attention to what is said and done. They observe the small details of every day life and attend to step by step experience. They prefer to let the eyes tell the mind.

Thinking and feeling

Thinking and feeling describe the two preferences associated with the *judging process*. They describe different preferences by which decisions are reached. Individuals who prefer thinking make decisions by objective, logical analysis. Individuals who prefer feeling make decisions by subjective values based on how people will be affected.

Individuals with a preference for thinking develop clear powers of analysis. They develop the ability to weigh facts objectively, and to predict consequences, both intended and unintended. They develop a stance of impartiality. They are characterised by a sense of fairness and justice and by the skill of applying logical analysis.

Individuals with a preference for thinking are good at putting things in logical order. They are also able to put people in their place when they consider it necessary. They are able to take tough decisions and to reprimand others. They are also able to be firm and tough-minded about themselves.

Thinking types need to be treated fairly and to see that other people are treated fairly as well. They are inclined to respond more to other people's ideas than to other people's feelings. They may inadvertently hurt other people's feelings without recognising that they are doing so.

Thinking types are able to anticipate and predict the logical outcomes of other people's choices. They can see the humour rather than the human pain in bad choices and wrong decisions taken by others. Thinking types prefer to look at life from the outside as a spectator.

Thinking types are able to develop good powers of logical analysis. They use objective and impersonal criteria at reaching decisions. They follow logically the relationships between cause and effect. They develop characteristics of being firm-minded and prizing logical order. They may appear sceptical.

Individuals who prefer feeling develop a personal emphasis on values and standards. They appreciate what matters most to themselves and what matters most to other people. They develop an understanding of people a wish to affiliate with people and a desire for harmony. They are characterised by their capacity for warmth, and by qualities of empathy and compassion.

Individuals with a preference for feeling like harmony and will work hard to bring harmony about between other people. They dislike telling other people unpleasant things or reprimanding other people. They take into account other people's feelings.

Feeling types need to have their own feelings recognised as well. They need praise and affirmation. They are good at seeing the personal effects of choices on their own lives and on other people's lives as well.

Feeling types are sympathetic individuals. They take a great interest in the people behind the job and respond to other people's values as much as to their ideas. They enjoy pleasing people.

Feeling types look at life from the inside. They live life as a committed participant and find it less easy to stand back and to form an objective view of what is taking place.

Feeling types develop good skills at applying personal priorities. They are good at weighing human values and motives, both their own and other people's. They are characterised by the qualities of empathy and sympathy. They prize harmony and trust.

Judging and perceiving

Judging and perceiving describe the two preferred attitudes towards the outer world. Individuals who prefer to relate to the outer world with a judging process present a planned and orderly approach to life. They prefer to have a settled system in place and display a preference for closure. Individuals who prefer to relate to the outer world with a perceiving process present a flexible and spontaneous approach to life. They prefer to keep plans and organisations to a minimum and display a preference for openness.

Judging types schedule projects so that each step gets done on time. They like to get things finished and settled, and to know that the finished product is in place. They work best when they can plan their work in advance and follow that plan. Judging types use lists and agendas to structure their day and to plan their actions. They may dislike interruption from the plans they have made and are reluctant to leave the task in hand even when something more urgent arises. Judging types tend to be satisfied once they reach a judgement or have made a decision, both about people and things. They dislike having to revise their decision and taking fresh information into account. They like to get on with a task as soon as possible once the essential things are at hand. As a consequence, judging types may decide to act too quickly.

When individuals taking a judging attitude towards the outer world, they are using the preferred *judging process*, thinking or feeling outwardly. Their attitude to life is characterised by deciding and planning, organising and scheduling, controlling and regulating. Their life is goal-orientated. They want to move towards closure, even when the data are incomplete.

Perceiving types adapt well to changing situations. They make allowances for new information and for changes in the situation in which they are living or acting. They may have trouble making decisions, feeling that they have never quite got enough information on which to base their decision.

Perceiving types may start too many projects and consequently have difficulty in finishing them. They may tend to postpone unpleasant tasks and to give their attention to more pleasant options. Perceiving types want to know all about a new task before they begin it, and may prefer to postpone something new while they continue to explore the options.

When perceiving types use lists they do so not as a way of organising the details of their day, but of seeing the possibilities in front of them. They may choose never to act on these possibilities. Perceiving types do not mind leaving things open for last minute changes. They work best under pressure and get a lot accomplished at the last minute under the pressure of a deadline.

When individuals take a perceiving attitude towards the outer world, they are using the preferred *perceiving process*, sensing or intuition, outwardly. They are taking in information, adapting and changing, curious and interested. They adopt an open minded attitude towards life and resist closure to obtain more data.

Dominant and inferior

According to Jung's theory every balanced individual needs to be able to command all four preferences or functions. We need *sensing* to gather all the relevant facts. We need *intuition* to see all measures that could be usefully taken. We need *thinking* to determine the consequences. We need *feeling* to consider the impact of these consequences on the people involved.

At the same time every balanced individual needs to develop one of these functions more than the others. This is the *dominant* function which gives each individual his or her defining characteristic. The dominant S shapes the practical person. The dominant N shapes the imaginative person. The dominant T shapes the logical person. The dominant F shapes the humane person.

The introvert prefers to exercise the dominant function within the inner world. The extrovert prefers to exercise the dominant function within the outer world.

Alongside the dominant function every balanced individual needs to develop a second prominent or *auxiliary* function. If the dominant function is associated with the perceiving process (sensing or intuition), the auxiliary function is associated with the judging process (thinking or feeling). If the dominant function is associated with the judging process (thinking or feeling), the auxiliary function is associated with the perceiving process (sensing or intuition).

The introvert prefers to employ the auxiliary function to relate to the outer world, leaving the dominant function free to deal with the inner world. The extrovert prefers to employ the auxiliary function to relate to the inner world, leaving the dominant function free to deal with the outer world.

The consequence of this difference is that when we meet extroverts we come face to face with their dominant characteristic. When we meet introverts we come face to face with their auxiliary characteristic. Introverts take longer to get to know and may appear withdrawn to extroverts. At the same time extroverts may appear shallow to introverts.

The cost of developing the dominant function is that the opposite function remains especially underdeveloped. This is known as the *inferior* function. Thus dominant thinking is paired with inferior feeling, while dominant feeling is paired with inferior thinking. Similarly dominant sensing is paired with inferior intuition, while dominant intuition is paired with inferior sensing.

The weakness of the inferior function is often exacerbated under pressure, stress or exhaustion. For example, when unduly tired, the person for whom thinking is dominant may misread or overlook the human values in a situation, the person for whom feeling is dominant may act illogically, the person for whom intuition is dominant may fail to see the obvious facts and pieces of data, and the person for whom sensing is dominant may fail to perceive the obvious links and relationships between and within the data.

While the dominant function is balanced by the inferior function, the auxiliary function is balanced by the *tertiary* function. Like the inferior function the tertiary function is less well developed, although generally not so underdeveloped as the inferior function. Once again the weakness of the tertiary function may be emphasised under pressure, stress or exhaustion.

Types and traits

Two very different traditions exist in personality psychology between models of personality which speak in terms of *types* and models of personality which speak in terms of *traits*. The Myers Briggs Type Indicator belongs to the first of these approaches and sets out to indicate psychological types. The difference between theories concerned with personality types and theories concerned with personality traits is most clearly illustrated by contrasting the Myers Briggs Type Indicator (which is concerned with personality types) with the Eysenck Personality Questionnaire (which is concerned with personality traits).

Confusion sets in immediately when the Myers Briggs Type Indicator and the Eysenck Personality Questionnaire employ the same language to describe aspects of their very different theories. Both talk in terms of extroversion and introversion.

According to trait theory, there is a continuum between extreme introversion and extreme extroversion. A single score on this trait scale locates each individual on this continuum. Individuals may be compared as being more or less extroverted, more or less introverted. On such a scale there is not clear boundary between where introversion ends and extroversion begins.

According to type theory there is a clear discontinuity between extroversion and introversion. An individual is clearly typed as indicating a preference for either introversion or for extroversion. A clear boundary exists between these two type preferences. While individuals may vary in the clarity with which they perceive and express their preference, the individual with a weak preference for extroversion has more in common with the individual who has a strong preference for extroversion than with an individual who has a weak preference for introversion.

Criticisms

The foregoing sections have attempted to set clearly the claims of the Myers Briggs Type Indicator as seen by the proponents of the theory. The theory is not, however, without formidable criticism among psychologists themselves. Such criticisms can best be summarised under five main headings.

First, the fundamental view that the individual differences can be accounted for in terms of two basic processes is regarded as very vulnerable. This view has its origins in Jung's description of psychological type, but it has never been proved by the objective tools of scientific psychology. For proponents of the Myers Briggs Type theory this starting point remains an essential tenet of belief. If the belief is found to be misplaced or inaccurate, the theory and its applications crumble.

Second, the technical debate in psychology between personality *types* and personality *traits* offers significant challenges to the very notion of a type indicator. According to trait theory what counts is an individual's position on a personality continuum, not the designation of a personality type. For example, trait theory challenges the view that individuals may be classified clearly into introverts or extroverts. Rather what may be clearly established is that individuals differ in the *degree* of introversion or extroversion which they display.

Third, the type indicator itself has been criticised for not reaching the generally accepted standards demanded of psychological test instruments. The two key criteria demanded of psychological tests are *validity* and *reliability*. Tests of validity assess the extent to which instruments actually measure what they set out to measure. Tests of reliability assess the extent to which the scores generated by measuring instruments are stable and consistent. Some empirical assessments of the indicator question these essential psychometric properties.

Fourth, there is still an important lack in the psychological literature of serious research studies scrutinising the robustness of the theory and its ability to predict practical outcomes. In view of this lack, the wise conclusion is not to dismiss the indicator, but to caution that the scientific evidence for its use is far from secure. More fundamental research is clearly and urgently needed. Meanwhile, the general consensus among personality psychologists remains very sceptical about the incomes of such research actually supporting the theory.

Fifth, some psychologists would be critical of the way in which individuals may become 'qualified' practitioners of the Myers Briggs Type Indicator. The test publishers in the UK require attendance at a five day training workshop after which standards are assessed by a multiple choice test examination. No prior psychological training is required before admission to the training workshop. Many of the qualified test users who apply the Myers Briggs Type Indicator theory in a religious context are not qualified psychologists. Two dangers may result from this. There may be a tendency to accept the theory in an uncritical fundamentalist fashion. There may be a tendency to incorporate within the theory ideas drawn in an undisciplined way from a wider eclectic field generally concerned with the relationships between spirituality and psychology conceived in the broadest of senses. The Myers Briggs Type Indicator should not be confused with the Enneagram or even the Keirsey and Bates theory of temperament styles.

In spite of these criticisms, there is also sufficient general support for the Myers Briggs Type Indicator in the psychological literature to sustain its continued use by the churches. Like all good psychological theories and instruments, the Myers Briggs Type Indicator may benefit from continued research and application. It is against this background that the second part of the paper sets the theory to work in relationship to the parable of the Prodigal Son.

The voice of scripture

Jesus told a story about a father who had two sons.

'The younger of the two sons said to his father, "Father, give me the share of property that falls to me." And he divided his living between them. Not many days later, the younger son gathered all he had and took his journey into a far country, and there he squandered his property in loose living. And when he had spent everything, a great famine arose in that country, and he began to be in want. So he went and joined himself to one of the citizens of that country, who sent him into his fields to feed swine. And he would gladly have fed on the pods that the swine ate; and no one gave him anything. But when he came to himself he said, "How many of the father's hired servants have bread enough and to spare, but I perish here with hunger! I will arise and go to my father, and I will say to him, "Father, I have sinned against heaven and before you; I am no longer worthy to be called your son; treat me as one of your hired servants."'

'And he arose and came to his father. But while he was yet at a distance, his father saw him and had compassion, and ran and embraced him and kissed him. And the son said to him, "Father, I have sinned against heaven and before you; I am no longer worthy to be called you son." But the father said to his servants, "Bring quickly the best robe, and put it on him; and put a ring on his hand, and shoes on his feet; and bring the fatted calf and kill it, and let us eat and make merry; for this my son was dead, and is alive again; he was lots, and is found." And they began to make merry.'

'Now the elder son was in the field; and as he came and drew near to the house, he heard music and dancing. And he called one of the servants and asked what this meant. And he said to him, "Your brother has come, and your father has killed the fatted calf, because

he has received him safe and sound." But he was angry and refused to go in. His father came out and entreated him, but he answered his father, "Lo, these many years I have served you, and I never disobeyed your command; yet you never gave me a kid, that I might make merry with my friends. But when this son of yours came, who has devoured your living with harlots, you killed for him the fatted calf!" And he said to him, "Son, you are always with me, and all that is mine is yours. It was fitting to make merry and be glad, for this your brother was dead, and is alive; he was lost, and is found."'

Personality and scripture
Introversion and extroversion
It is all too easy for introverts and extroverts to misunderstand each other. To the introvert, extroverts appear noisy, shallow, brash and loud. To the extrovert, introverts appear silent, withdrawn, moody and quiet. When extroverts face a major decision, they need to talk with others about it, and to act quickly. When introverts face a major decision, they need to withdraw from others and to think long before acting . No wonder introverts and extroverts misunderstand each other.

Jesus of Nazareth was well aware of the difficulties which introverts and extroverts experience when they live together. Jesus said, 'There was a man who had two sons: one was an introvert and one was an extrovert.' The younger son was clearly an extrovert and the older son was clearly an introvert. No wonder there was so much conflict in that family.

As an extrovert, the younger son craved for the excitement of the outer world. He longed for the stimulation of people. He sought for the sounds of society. He yearned for conversation and for other people with whom to share his ideas, his energy, his enthusiasm.

As an extrovert, he tired of the closed in environment of the farm. He was frustrated by the emptiness of isolation. He was exhausted by the silence of solitude. He was driven to distraction by the lack of company and by the absence of new people with whom he could relate.

So he went off to seek new places and new people. He went out of his way to experience life as widely as possible and to savour the richness of the outer world.

As an introvert, the older son craved for the excitement of the inner world. He longed for the stimulation of isolation. He sought for the silence of solitude. He yearned for space away from other people to ponder his ideas, to recharge his energy, to sharpen his enthusiasm. As an introvert, he avoided the excitement of the outer world. He shunned the stimulation of people. He distrusted the sounds of society. he was driven to distraction by his brother's insatiable quest for company and for conversation.

He was totally content to stay on the farm with the small number of people whom he really knew, friends whom he really trusted. He stayed at home to experience life as deeply as possible and to savour the richness of the inner world.

Jesus of Nazareth said, 'There was a man who had two sons: one was an introvert and one was an extrovert.' Little wonder they found it difficult to understand each other's orientation to life. But their father loved them both. In the same way our God loves and accepts the introvert and the extrovert. For both there is a place in the Kingdom of God.

Sensing and intuition

It is all too easy for intuitive people and sensing people to misunderstand each other. To the intuitive person, sensing types appear unimaginative, boring, small minded and unnecessarily cautious. To the sensing person, intuitive types appear impractical, day dreamers, undisciplined. When intuitives face a new situation, they allow the mind to inform their eyes. When sensing people face a new situation, they allow their eyes to inform the mind. No wonder sensing people and intuitive people misunderstand each other.

Jesus of Nazareth was well aware of the difficulties which sensing people and intuitive people experience when the live together. Jesus said, 'There was a man who had two sons: one was an intuitive type and the other a sensing type.' The younger son was clearly an intuitive person and the older son was clearly a sensing person. No wonder there was so much conflict in the family.

As an intuitive type, the younger son was a visionary who was always alert to the unseen possibilities around the next corner. He was a man who preferred to trust his insight into the future; a man who could be relied upon for spotting new possibilities and trying out new things.

As an intuitive person, he became restless with the relentless routine of life on the farm. He became bored with the constant rehearsal of familiar pattern. He tired of counting the calves in the field.

So he looked at his share of the farm and instantly visualised what its value could purchase in the markets of the town. He saw no loss in leaving the past behind.

As a sensing person, the older son was a practical man who was content to live with the reality of the present moment. He was a man who preferred to trust what he knew from past experience; a man who could be relied upon to know how many calves were in the field.

As a sensing person, he saw little point in speculating about the unseen possibilities waiting around the next corner. He placed no confidence in untested future possibilities. He was not interested in trying out new ideas.

He looked at his share of the farm and loved every familiar detail; he wanted it all to remain unchanged. He saw every loss in leaving the past behind.

Jesus of Nazareth said, 'There was a man who had two sons: one was an intuitive person, and one was a sensing person.' Little wonder they found it difficult to understand each other's way of looking at life. But their father loved them both. In the same way our God loves and accepts the intuitive person and the sensing person. For both there is a place in the Kingdom of God.

Thinking and feeling

It is all too easy for thinking people and feeling people to misunderstand each other. To the thinker, the feeling person appears illogical, indecisive, and far too tenderminded. To the feeling person, the thinker appears inhumane, cold, and far too tough-minded. When thinking types face a new decision, their first concern is to weigh up all the facts as dispassionately as possible. When feeling types face a new decision, their first concern is to ask how people's lives will be affected. No wonder thinking types and feeling types misunderstand each other.

Jesus of Nazareth was well aware of the difficulties which thinking types and feeling types experience when they live together. Jesus said, 'There was a man who had two sons: one was a feeling type and the other was a thinking type.' The younger son was clearly a thinking person and the older son was clearly a feeling person. No wonder there was so much conflict in the family.

As a thinking person, the younger son made his decisions in life on the basis of clear cold logic. He carefully weighed the pros and the cons and came to a balanced objective judgement. He argued for fairness and for autonomy.

As a thinking person, he saw other people's feelings as secondary to logical analysis. He saw human subjectivity as a sign of softness and weakness. He felt constrained by pleas for harmony and for independence.

So he looked at the logic of dividing the inheritance, but never thought how his action would affect the lives of the father and of the brother. He looked at the logic of returning home, but never thought of the emotional impact of his return on the lives of others.

As a feeling, person, the older son made his decisions in life on the basis of how other people would be affected. He carefully weighed the human values involved and came to a humane subjective judgement. He argued for harmony and for interdependence.

As a feeling person, he saw logical analysis as cold, clinical and inhumane. He saw balanced objectivity as a sign of toughness and heartlessness. He felt constrained by pleas for fairness and for autonomy. So he felt the hurt in his own life; he felt the hurt in the father's life when the brother walked out. He felt the resentment at the brother's return, but never thought of the logic of the lost being found.

Jesus of Nazareth said, 'There was a man who had two sons: one was a thinking person and one was a feeling person.' Little wonder they found it difficult to understand each other's criteria in making the decisions of life. But their father loved them both. In the same way our God loves and accepts the thinking person and the feeling person. For both there is a place in the Kingdom of God.

Judging and perceiving

It is all too easy for individuals who prefer to present their judging process to the outer world and for individuals who prefer to present their perceiving process to the outer world to misunderstand each other. To the judging person, the perceiver appears disorganised, chaotic and downright irresponsible. To the perceiving person, the judger appears rigid, inflexible and obsessed with the constraints of structure and time. When the judging types consider a day out they begin by formulating a timetable and a disciplined programmed, but may miss the most exciting possibilities. When perceiving types consider a day out, they begin by brainstorming all the things they could do, but may never quite get round to doing them. When judging types face a choice, they want the matter settled and closed. When perceiving types face a choice, they want to keep the options open and flexible for as long as possible.

Jesus of Nazareth was well aware of the difficulties which judging types and perceiving types experience when they live together. Jesus said, 'There was a man who had two sons: one was a judging type and the other was a perceiving type'. The younger son was clearly a perceiving person and the older son was clearly a judging person. No wonder there was so much conflict in the family.

As a perceiving person, the younger son felt constrained by the regular rhythm of the family home. He was bored by the unaltering pattern of life on the farm.

As a perceiving person, he longed for the freedom and flexibility of spontaneity. He wanted to respond to the new opportunities and to the new possibilities of each unfolding situation.

So he looked for the chance to turn his back on the life he had known so well and to break free from the constraints imposed by the expectations of the family and farm. He adapted well to the new life of luxury in the town, to the way of poverty in the time of famine, and to the restoration to the family home.

As a judging person, the older son felt disorientated by the changing expectations of his brother. He was amazed by the lack of predictability and by the sea of uncertainty.

As a judging person, he longed for the stability of the family home, for the familiarity of structure and for the predictability of routine. He missed the friendly presence of the fatted calf in the family field. He wanted longer notice of the family party.

So he dug in his heels and refused to change his mind. He continued living the life which he had planned and refused to welcome changing circumstances.

Jesus of Nazareth said, 'There was a man who had two sons, one son was a judging person and one was a perceiving person.' Little wonder they found it difficult to understand each other's attitude toward the outer world. But their father loved them both. In the same, our God loves and accepts the judging person and the perceiving person. For both there is a place in the Kingdom of God.

Postscript

In the language of the Myers Briggs Type Indicator, the younger son was an ENTP and the older son was an ISFJ. As such they were complete opposites. As well as affirming the father's acceptance of both sons, the parable of Jesus highlights the weaknesses in both sons.

In their own ways, both sons are guilty of being inconsiderate, self-centred, and selfish. Both sons fail to see life from the perspective favoured by the opposite personality type. While the Myers Briggs Type Indicator may help to explain human behaviour, it does not seek to excuse it. By offering insight into human behaviour, however, the Myers Briggs Type Indicator does empower individuals both to name their strengths and to work on their weaknesses. Through his teaching, Jesus the psychologist also offered insight into human behaviour. Through his death and resurrection, Jesus the Saviour transformed and refashioned us in his own image. Pray, then, that we may be both informed by Jesus the teacher and transformed by Jesus the Saviour.

Further reading

R. Bayne, *The Myers-Briggs Type Indicator: a critical review and practical guide*, London, Chapman and Hall, 1995.

I. Briggs-Myers and P.B. Myers, *Gifts Differing*, Palo Alto, CA, Consulting Psychologists Press, 1980.

C.Bryant, *Jung and the Christian Way*, London, Darton, Longman and Todd, 1983.

B. Duncan, *Pray Your Way: your personality and God*, London, Darton, Longman and Todd, 1993.

M. Goldsmith, *Knowing Me: knowing God*, London, Triangle, 1994.

M. Goldsmith, and M. Wharton, *Knowing Me, Knowing You*, London SPCK, 1993.

C.J. Keating, *Who We Are is How We Pray*, Mystic, CT, Twenty-Third Publications, 1987.

O. Kroeger and J.M. Thuesen, *Type Talk*, New York, Delta, 1988.

O. Kroeger and J.M. Thuesen, *Type Talk at Work*, New York, Delacorte Press, 1992.

C.P. Michael and M.C. Morrisey, *Prayer and Temperament*, Charlotttesville, Virginia, The Open Book Inc., 1984.

S. Moss, *Jungian Typology*, Melbourne, Collins Dove, 1989.

L. Osborn and D. Osborn, *God's Diverse People*, London, Daybreak, 1991.

R.M. Oswald and O. Kroeger, *Personality Type and Religious Leadership*, Washington, DC, Alban Institute, 1988.

A. Thorne and H. Gough, *Portraits of Type*, Palo Alto, CA, Consulting Psychologists Press, 1991.

I. Williams, *Prayer and My Personality*, Bramcote, Grove Books, 1987.

Sermon
Rev. Stuart W. Roebuck

Text:
"...though you do not now see him you believe in him and rejoice with an unutterable and exalted joy."
                                                                    1 Peter 1:8b (RSV).

Introduction
A very stuffy and pompous Lord of the Manor was out walking his dog on his large estate one morning, when he happened to meet a young hiker who was hopelessly lost in the woods. The hiker had no idea that he was addressing a member of the House of Lords. "Morning, mate, " he said, "Can you tell me where this path goes to?" "Young man," huffed and puffed the Lord of the Manor, full of indignation at the hiker's brashness, "Don't you know who you're talking to?:" "Well, there's a coincidence," said the young hiker. "I don't know where I'm going and you don't know who you are!"
As long as human beings have been self-conscious and capable of reflective thought, I would guess that those two admissions of ignorance have been common human properties. "Who am I, and where am I going?" If a lively imagination gives any kind of proof, I can hear those questions being pondered by people in every generation in our islands, Blue-painted Celts, medieval peasants, Victorian factory slaves, modern inhabitants of the urban sprawl. Only the successful and self-confident might have been too busy to hear that still small voice of human anxiety; "Who am I, and where am I going?"

Part One: "... though you do not now see him"
For centuries people have turned to religion to find answers to questions of that kind. In recent times they have turned to science as well. And so the Christ and the Cosmos Initiative was formed for people like you and me who want to reject the discoveries of neither religion nor science, but to harmonise whatever is relevant in both

disciplines. It seems years ago now that the team, groping towards a brief expression of the Initiative's purpose, accepted this formula as our key question: *What has science revealed that might make difference to our theology or the way we express it?*
I can imagine the disciple Thomas being very much at home in our company. Doubting Thomas? How unfair! He reacted on Easter Day in just the way any one of us would have reacted in his shoes. "Come on, friends. You can't expect me to believe in something so far beyond our normal experience without some kind of evidence. Show me the proof, then I'll believe it." That was not a faithless or irreligious approach, it was normal, cautious, sensitive questioning of the kind we would appreciate and approve of any claim about a unique supernatural event. We have learned from one another through these nine years of the Initiative to be hesitant about our certainties.

One thing which more than any other prevents an advancement of learning is the belief that you already know all there is to know, or at least you think you know all you need to know. A closed mind, no matter how brilliant, is incapable of growing in understanding beyond certain fixed points. Let me give you an illustration.

A little while ago I read a poem by Elizabeth Barrett Browning. the poem filled a whole book, and the book was 377 pages long. I was amazed that anyone could write so much and say so little, though one or two bits are quite good, as any fellow-Philistine will confirm. The poem was called "Aurora Leigh", the name of its central character. She was an orphaned child, half English and half Italian. She was born in Italy, but when her parents died she was sent to live in England with her father's sister. This woman was well-intentioned and virtuous, but narrow and unemotional, satisfied by the trivialities of middle class manners, nurtured and moulded by Victorian England. Elizabeth Barrett Browning described her in these words:

She had lived a sort of cage-bird life, born in a cage,
accounting that to leap from perch to perch
was act and joy enough for any bird.
Dear heaven, how silly are the things that live
in thickets, and eat berries.

How often Church activity has seemed in the past to be no more than leaping from perch to perch, frantic journeying which goes nowhere. Perhaps life in the laboratory sometimes feels like that too. The Initiative has pushed open the cage-bird's door and we have learned to enjoy a wilder theology. Fresh air blows through the thickets where scientific religious beliefs are tangled together, and what once seemed insurmountable obstacles to faith and reason have withered away. I leave the image with you; pushing a metaphor too far can spoil it.

Part Two: "... though you do not now seem him you believe in him"

So the first stage in my argument is that the Initiative's work has been concerned with removing obstacles to faith. Not that the work is finished, of course. Half an hour in a classroom with any bunch of teenagers will convince you that anti-religious prejudice is alive and well. Belief in science as the only answer to all things is still the norm. But at least you and I are a little further along the road than that.

My study back at the Manse was decorated a few weeks ago. All the books files, furniture, curtains, lampshades and junk came out. On went new wallpaper and fresh-smelling paint. What a delight it was, cleared of all the obstacles to tidiness. I longed to keep it like that, clean and empty, though it would not have been much use as a study in that state.

Nor do you create faith merely by clearing away the obstacles to it. Faith is not an empty room. Clearing the obstacles is very important, getting rid of unnecessary clutter, but for faith to be of any use it has to be furnished with beliefs.

How do we furnish this empty room of faith? Which new furnishings has the science and religion debate contributed in recent years? *"Has science revealed which might make a difference to our theology or the way we express it?"* Science has revealed that the universe is much bigger, much older, much more complicated, much more understandable, and much more beautiful than we had ever imagined. The difference it makes to our theology is the realisation that God who planned and sustains it and who became incarnate in Jesus Christ is also infinitely greater in every way than we had previously understood. A creator and saviour whom we can only acknowledge as Lord and God.

Do you remember that famous saying from Isaac Newton about his early days? I've heard it more than once in our previous conferences. Isaac Newton said that he had been like a boy wandering on the seashore, delighting every now and then in a particularly interesting pebble or beautiful shell, but quite unaware that the great sea of knowledge lay before him unexplored.

Perhaps we are still like children on the seashore, pausing every now and then to delight in some small aspect of creation, not because we are unaware of the vast sea of knowledge waiting to be explored, but because we know that exploring all of it is quite beyond the capability of any one of us. But that admission of ignorance is in no way a statement of despair. Christianity is a community of faith. It isn't necessary for every individual to understand in detail every arcane corner of knowledge. What we have instead is a reasonable faith, a confidence that scientific and religious interpretations of the universe are inextricably intertwined, the ability to see the profound in the ordinary, and the belief - to quote Elizabeth Barrett Browning again - the belief that it is possible to see every common bush aflame with God.

Part Three: "... though you do not now see him you believe in him and rejoice with an unutterable and exalted joy."
So the recent science and religion debate has not only cleared away obstacles to faith, but also magnified the content of faith. The final area to think about is that of human needs and emotions.

On television three or four weeks ago there was a ten minute film from Russia. It was the story of two elderly sisters who lived some distance apart, one going to visit the other for a few days in winter. The film revealed lives of unremitting poverty and hardship, in which the exchange of a little butter and a few potatoes were luxuries which made existence possible. The transforming ten seconds in the film occurred when one of the sisters went to a service in an Orthodox church. Standing in the crowd, watching the rich ceremony, listening to the beautiful music, she said "Only in Church is my soul at rest."

The questions "Who am I?" and "Where am I going?" are profound questions about the nature of human life which require the detailed reasoned answers and arguments which scientists and theologians try to give. But the questions are also more than that. They are a cry from the heart. They need replies which satisfy the emotions as well as the mind.

We might find new paths of thought and better modes of expression through the science and religion debate, but the destination is still much as it ever was. Religion is not without purpose, and faith is not an empty room. We need to have faith in the worth of each individual life, and a trust that high ideals and moral values and self-sacrifice are not delusions. We need to believe that there really is forgiveness for our failures, victory over suffering and comfort for sorrows. And we need to believe that even death does not nullify and extinguish the purpose and value of life, and that in the Church (or at least in God's presence) our souls can be at rest. Without knowing all the answers, and without being able to follow all the arguments, we might still be able through faith to resolve the questions and to rejoice with an unutterable and exalted joy.

Conclusion

Back to Thomas and the story on John's Gospel. Even eight days after the resurrection Thomas still knew very little. His future was shrouded in mystery, even as for us Thomas' life is still shrouded in legend. But what he did know was enough for the time being. His reasonable questioning was answered, and he was able to make that great statement of faith in the Risen Christ, "My Lord and my God."

"... though you do not now see him you believe in him and rejoice with unutterable and exalted joy."

No returning for Thomas to the Upper Room, any more than Moses returned to look for the burning bush or St. Paul kept on going back to the Damascus Road or John Wesley to Aldersgate Street. The experience had been profound, but was once and for all. Now it was time to look to the future. He was at the beginning of the next adventure.

Amen.

PART TWO
Discussions

REPORT ON WORK SESSION

This streamed group was led by Dr. K. Bertie Everard; there were 23 members. We started by separately filling in a questionnaire identifying 45 trends that influence the worlf of work and marking each on a scale of 0 to 4, to identify trends which were most pronounced (4) or least descerable (0). Individuals then identified 10 trends which they considered to be most appropriate for a clear Christian response. The group then came together to discuss its findings.

The 10 top scorers from the group as a whole for focussing a Christian response included 5 trends which were directly or closely associated with the problems posed by unemployment, and this became the dominant issue discussed by the group for the rest of the session.

The conversation quickly became polarised; some members lay the problem of unemployment firmly at the door of unsympathetic management treating employees as 'things' rather than people and ruthlessly 'downsizing' to maximise profits, whilst other members argued that the economic circumstances facing business gave the employers and managers few alternative options. It was recognised that both those made redundant and those managing an enterprise faced high levels of stress which needed to be recognised and addressed by the church.

The consensus of the group was that the problem of unemployment was a cultural problem of society which was the result of different pressures including the short-term pressures from 'the city' and the growth of low wage economies in the rising third world.

What can be done?

In times of upheaval in a company, there was a desperate need for good communication to ensure that the workforce understood the problems faced by management and that management understood the effect of its actions on the workforce.

Changed oganisational structures with flatter hierarchical forms led directly to better communication and, potentially, lower management overheads.
The national education system need to recognise the problems faced by its teenage output, many of whom went straight on to social security. There was still a tendency for schools to train young people to fill roles that no longer existed. It was important to train young school leavers to face the realities and uncertainties of the world which they were about to enter.

A Christian response
- These people are my brothers and sisters, I must look after them.
- New opportunities for job creation must be found, for instance in leisure areas.
- Some advocated that the pain should be shared by all members of a work-force agreeing to take a percentage cut in wages to keep the wage bill constant without the need to shed jobs; others pointed out that this would raise problems within the trade union movement.
- Christian churches should establish support groups for people facing redundancy.
- One member of the group described a local 'Faith in the Modern World' initiative that sought to apply political pressure through lobbying Mps.
- One member drew the groups attention to a Baptist Church in Cambridge that has established a work area offering training and employment to young people out of work.
- It was suggested that people in stressful situations often need a 'Christian Listener' to share problems with.
- More use could be made of training in 'problem-solving' to assist young people in coping with unstructured situations - as offered, for example by the YMCA.

Conclusion
This was a challenging issue. It would be facile to give the impression that the group arrived at any satisfactory solutions bu the discussion stimulated it to consider, in a Christian context, what is the most critical work-related issue of our age: the debilitating problem of those who want to work but are unable to find a job.

CHILDREN IN THE FAMILY

Leader - Linda Gow, Clinical Psychologist currently full-time mother.

Mrs. Gow suggested we looked at the life cycle of the family and how a network of Christian faith and professionalism (psychology) can come together in an attempt to help families with and the various problems which confront them; for example emotional, social and relationship problems, suicide, eating problems, abuse.
The aim is to show how psychology and Christianity are compatible and complimentary and that even a rudimentary understanding of psychology is highly relevant and can enrich our faith and our ability to understand and respond appropriately and with sensitivity to the needs of those within and without our church fellowships.

A. Biblical Model of Family.
B. Family Life Cycle - a Psychological Model of the Family.
C. Unexpected/Undesirable Life Events
D. Different Family Models.
E. Our/The Church's Response to:
  1. Preserving God's ideal for family life/
  2. Those experiencing unexpected life events or from different family models to our own?

A. BIBLICAL MODEL OF FAMILY
Genesis 2 - pre-Fall - marriage is shown as creation ordinance - divine intention of God that couple come together and leave and cleave. Marriage seen as community of just two individuals (monogamous model). Hosiah's covenant with Israel, so with the marriage covenant - one man and one woman.
Genesis 1:28 - bearing children is encouraged, but after the Fall a woman will experience pain in labour.

The Bible gives evidence of God's love for children. He saw children as important, as individuals in their own right, not as possessions.
Matthew 18:3-4 Jesus said: ....except ye turn and become as little children, ye shall in no wise enter into the kingdom of heaven. Whosoever therefore shall humble himself as this little child, the same is the greatest in the kingdom of heaven.
Mark 10:13-16... Suffer the little children to come unto me....
Ephesians 6:1-4 the relationship between parents and children.
Children, obey your parents in the Lord: for this is right. Honour thy father and mother (which is the first commandment with promise). That it may be well with thee, and thou mayest live long on the earth. And, ye fathers, provoke not your children to wrath: but nurture them in the chastening and admonition of the Lord.
Colossians 3:20-21 relates to responsibility of parents to encourage their children.
Children, obey your parents in all things, for this is well pleasing in the Lord. Fathers, provoke not your children, that they be not discouraged.
1 Timothy 3:4-5 talking to those in authority in the church who have families:
One that ruleth well his own house, having his children in subjection with all gravity; (But if a man knoweth not how to rule his own house, how shall he take care of the church of God?)
The relationship between husband and wife is seen as 'different, but equal'.
Genesis 2:18-25 no indication that men are superior to women, but complimentary roles to play.
1 Cor. 13: defines love)   Marriage service
Col. 3:13-17
Ephesians 5:22-23: (Roles):
Wives be in subjection unto your own husbands, as unto the Lord. For the husband is the head of the wife, as Christ also is the head of the church, being himself the saviour of the body.

Outlines the argument for headship model for family life and supports patriarchal society - man is in authority in the family.
Divorce/Remarriage - complex
Deut. 24:1-4
Matthew 5:31-32
Matthew 19:1-9
1 Cor. 7:15 Desertion
Phil. 2:3 Power
James 2:12 Mercy over judgement
God's ideal is a monogamous relationship. God advocates mercy, repentance, full forgiveness and a new start, but his Church does not always see it that way and often judges. The Church of England generally does not remarry people in Church, but gives a Blessing on account of the fact that there has been a previous marriage. God's point of view is that of repentance and receiving God's forgiveness; a blessing but no remarriage in church is a controversial issue.
James 2:13: For judgement is without mercy to him that have shewed no mercy: mercy glorieth against judgement.

B. WHAT DOES PSYCHOLOGY BRING TO OUR UNDERSTANDING OF THE FAMILY

(See Table 2)
This is a form we can use as a critical tool. Reading the sheet vertically are major transition points in life cycle.
1. Preparing for family (adolescence 15-20 years), becoming independent and leaving home, then 'meeting and cleaving' and forming a new unit.
2. Forming the new family.
3. From twosome to threesome.
4. Losses in family.
and so on.............
Reading the sheet horizontally gives the emotional processes that are likely for that stage; for example, accepting separation of parents and offspring.

The Church can offer the family sacraments - confirmation, marriage, baptism. Family life cycle is circular not horizontal and vertical - follows through the adolescent in the family to point of death. He/she becomes self-directing person wanting to experiment with own ideas, but still connected with family and under parental guidance. Difficulties arise when parents cannot let children go, if there are no compromises the result can be estrangement. Parents are trying to direct their children's lives and come into conflict over church attendance, and their children's questioning of parents' and the Church's values and beliefs.

Stage 2 successful transition. Marriage takes place resulting with a relationship between the two families with the possibility of the complexity of different beliefs and ideas. Sue Woodward Skinner gave figure of 49% divorces by fifth wedding anniversary due to severe marital problems - Britain = one in three marriages, United States of America = one in two marriages. Marriage entails compromise, fitting in with someone else; placing partner's needs over those of his/her parents.

Marriage ceremony is a public statement and ritual that couples go through which seals their relationship and commitment to each other. In a Christian marriage do they put God first, spouse second and family further down?

Third state parenthood - twosome to three, four, fivesome. Their parents are becoming grandparents, sisters and brothers aunts and uncles. Couple is now involved with wider community, for example with clinics, GPs, schools. The issue which arises is how to balance time between partner and children which can be stressful. A relationship has to be secure before thinking of having a child - 'happy family' with baby is a myth. Baptism is important in Church life - the child is given to God and the Church community. Mrs. Gow's husband, C of England curate, is often asked "What is the meaning of this?" (baptism) "What is the alternative?" She cited the case of unmarried parents who are accepted and belong in their church and often have their children baptised and co-opt couples as godparents to help child within the church.

Stage 4 adolescent families. Parents are often in mid-life crisis, reflecting on "what is happening with my life?"; going out and having a good time, indulging in extramarital affairs in their desire to be young and endearing again, or preparing for empty nest - "what are we going to do?" after looking after children for all those years, they cannot be parents again. At the same time adolescents are taking risks and there is concern for the health of the older generation.

Stage 5 extending family. The couple is faced with each other again. Communication can be a problem if they have used their children as a means of communicating with each other and find they do not know each other very well. There is an opportunity to indulge in related activities or maybe divorce resulting in either a new start or loneliness. There may be loss of elderly parents and the grieving process to contend with. New career or part-time work may be considered. The wife may have given up her job before marriage and been a full-time mother until the children were aged 15 or 16 years, she may consider working again. Stepfamilies may split up; children of both families may come together, or spouse may leave with his/her children. The church's role can be important in conciliation, reconciliation and healing. It can endorse second marriages instead of judging and criticising which results in these families feeling unsupported.

Stage 6 - reforming the family. The adolescent is now a grandparent whose children are taking responsibility for young and old members of the family. The ageing process results in a re-evaluation of spiritual matters which become important again. The Church provides spiritual refreshment and a social outlet.

Stage 7 - Transcending the family. Departure from this life means the end of a particular generation for family. Loss and death are the hallmarks of this stage. The Church can play its part as healing ministry, giving of last rites, and helping in the process of mourning. The process of mourning as a family is important and healing. A funeral can result in the mending of relationships, a family coming together, or tension in an enforced meeting, or an opportunity for sharing pain and loss of a loved relative. People open up to a curate when he takes a funeral and he can help people explore a faith.

Questions put to Mrs. Gow.

The Biblical model of family (St. Paul's model) with the wife promising to obey was culturally determined; society today has no equivalent model and we have not sorted out what that model should be.

Mrs. Gow - Scripture has been used to support patriarchal model with women's subservient role and not as ordained by God as an equal role. The word 'head' authority means <u>source</u> in Greek.

People who have studied the scriptures see God as a loving father yet own father was a Calvanist to whom God gave messages, yet he was a sincere man so we have to be grateful.

Mrs. Gow - the relationship of father, mother to children: 'children obey their parents', but parents must respect their children and not exasperate them. St. Paul made great advances in people's thinking. For example in the Jewish service a common prayer of men is to thank God for not creating him a slave or woman. Paul moved on from that attitude encouraging husbands to love and cherish their wives at a time when women and children had no value in society. Paul, a single man, believed that the Kingdom of God was coming so he was mainly preoccupied with evangelism and did not address the issue of slavery.

C. UNEXPECTED LIFE EVENTS
Childlessness (not by choice)
Unplanned pregnancy
Premature illness/death of children or adults

Separation/Divorce/Remarriage
Emotional/Physical/Sexual Abuse of Children or Adults.

D. DIFFERENT FAMILY FORMS
Single
Single parenthood through no partner or loss of partner
Reconstituted family (stepfamily)
Childless couple (not by choice)
Foster family

E. DISCUSSION
Questions:
Personal and church response to:
A. How do we ensure that God's ideal plan for family life is preserved for future generations?
B. What should our response be to those experiencing unexpected (perhaps undesirable) life events and/or from different family models to our own within and without our church fellowships?
(See sheets from board for answers:-
A Church family
Marriage/Baptism preparation
Education/Teaching - Mixing of groups (elderly, young etc.)
Supportive counselling
Healing ministry
Moral rigour
Pastoral compassion

Joan Roebuck

	Family life cycle stage	Emotional process of transition	Required relationship shift	Sacraments and occasional offices
1. Conception	Preparing for family Adolescence	Accepting parent/offspring separation	Differentation of self from family of origin. Development of intimate peer relationships. Establishment of self in work.	Confirmation
2. Birth	Young Adulthood Forming the family	Commitment to new system	Marital choices Forming the maritial relationship Realignment of relationships with extended families and friends to include spouse.	Marriage
3. Childhood	Young family Parenting	Accepting new members into system.	Moving from two-some to three-some and beyond. Taking on parenting roles. Realignment of relations with extended family to include paretning and grandparental roles.	Baptism
4. Adolescence	Mid Life Adolescent families	Increasing flexibility of family boundaries to inlcude children's independence.	Shifting parent/child relationships to permit adolescents to move in and out. Refocusing mid-life marital and career issues. Concern for older generation.	Confirmation/ Orders

5. Young Adulthood:	'Empty Nest' Extending the family Children leave home Menopause	Accepting multitude of exits from and entries into the family system.	Renegotiation back to marital dyad. Development of adult to adult relationships between parents and children. Realignment of relationships to include in-laws and grandchildren. Dealing with losses and partings through loss of children, death or divorce.	Conciliation/ reconciliation and healing.
6. Maturity	Re-forming the family. Later life.	Accepting the shift of generational and/or interfamilial roles.	Renegotiation of roles to enable central and/or to include the joining of 2 new family systems after re-marriage. Exploration of new social and familial options.	Eucharist
7. Completion	Transcending the family. Death	Accepting disintegration of family and ultimate detachment.	Dealing with loss of spouse, siblings and other peers. Making room for wisdom and dependency of older generation. New realism stemming from life review of unfulfilled hopes and ultimate goals. Preparing for death and new life.	Healing. Last rites and funeral office.

CHILDREN AT SCHOOL

Mrs. Gwyneth Little

We considered psychology and its relevance to the classroom and addressed three questions:
- What is the Christian view of children?
- What is the Christian view of education?
- What is the Christian view of the relationship between pupil and teacher?

Psychology offers a scientific way of evaluating concepts, of analysing the processes of learning and of assessing the effectiveness of methods. We considered, both by remembering our own time at school and by reflecting on our experience as adults, the way we ourselves learn and assimilate new material and what influences the effectiveness of our learning. We tried practical exercises involving the recall of words and the positive effect on both short and long term memory of recognising relevance and seeing a pattern and of motivation and the negative effect of factors like anxiety. We recognised the need to teach children how to learn and for teachers to understand how children make mistakes.

While within each age band we recognised a range of abilities it is clear that all children are proceeding through successive stages of various forms of development, both cognitive and moral, and various forms of assessment and measurement are current in each area of Kohlberg's stages of moral development on the one hand, and reading tests on the other; we recognised that there is a variety of data which can facilitate analysis and improvement in learning-centred teaching in the classroom.

We responded to our three questions as follows:
1. Each child is a special, unique individual and the gift of God.
2. The Christian view of education sees each child as a whole; it values truth and asserts the individual quality of each child; therefore equality of opportunity is to be sought for each child to

develop its own aptitudes and abilities, even though the present educational system makes this unlikely;. We noted the continuing need to avoid stereotyping because of gender or on other grounds, and also the needs of the increasing number of children who may lack support from home: there is no evidence that children need or value the love and support of parents any less than in the past; quite the contrary; and where this is not fully forthcoming extra burdens are laid both on the child and on the school.

3. The relationship between teacher and pupil should involve mutual trust and respect. The teacher is there to serve the needs of the learning child, and attitudes are all-important. Most important is the need for love, recognising that teacher and pupil belong to one family.

Clergy and Personality

Led by Rev. Prof. Leslie Francis. Chaired by Mrs. Stella Bristow.

Our discussion considered clergy personality types and compared them with those of lay people; the role of clergy and the satisfaction that is available within it, the use of personality tests in predicting the suitability of people for the role; the causes of stress and burn-out together with means of salvage.

The personality characteristics of clergy were discussed and Professor Francis made reference to his own observations of male and female clergy in England. He suggested that the basic differences between the sexes were an observed reality which was measurable and suggested that the male characteristics were extrovert and tough-minded and female characteristics were neurotic. We discussed the expectations that people had of clergy, whether they were stable or neurotic, emotional or unemotional, introvert or extrovert. The role of prayer and spirituality and tough-mindedness or tender-mindedness were discussed. The question was raised as to whether particular psychological types were attracted to ministry.

Professor Francis described his observations within the ministry of the Church of England and suggested that the majority of male ministers had psychological characteristics more like those of females, introvert, neurotic and tender-minded and he suggested that these were not suited to the public role so often required. He suggested that the female clergy had psychological types modelled on men in general, stable, tough-minded and extrovert.

The question of how far male and female traits depended on environment was discussed and whether society imposed such differences. Reference was made to experiments in which people were observed to treat infants that they thought were male in quite a different way to infants they thought were female. The babies which were assumed to be male were encouraged to be active and those which were assumed to be female encouraged to be passive, regardless of the true sex of the children. Some members of the group objected to the whole process of labelling people and others suggested that it was a call to ministry by God which mattered, not psychological type. It was agreed that there was a complication in reconciling the psychological analysis of people with divine call and gifts and graces. Professor Francis suggested that there was a tendency to confuse description with prescription. Selection boards tended to choose people like themselves and that they themselves were chosen by similar people. Much more variety of personality types was required in ministry. This mis-match of personality to expected role disabled much ministry. People were required to go against their own personality type, using much more energy leading to burn-out in the long term. He described research amongst clergy in Wales concerning the effects of ministry upon those engaged in it.

The clergy concerned were questioned about three categories; personal accomplishment, emotional exhaustion and de-personalisation.

Personal Accomplishment

	Feeling
64%	accomplishing worthwhile things
75%	exhilaration in working closely with parishioners
66%	having positive influence on other peoples lifes
90%	feel personal satisfaction from working with people
31%	deal effectively with parishioners
61%	feel empathy with parishioners
36%	feel energetic
84%	would follow the same calling again
79%	feel calm in dealing with problems

emotional exhaustion

9%	feel at the end of their tether
40%	worked too hard
15%	feel burned out
35%	feel frustrated
24%	found working with people all day a strain
17%	feel fatigued in the morning
47%	feel drained at the end of the day
5%	would want to leave the ministry
7%	found working with people too much stress

depersonalisation

26%	found themselves less patient
12%	found themselves callous to people

5%	could not be bothered to understand people
8%	wanted people to leave them alone
18%	found it difficult to listen to people
21%	found themselves hardening emotionally
31%	feel blamed by parishioners
0.6%	wanted help

It was found that the younger clergy suffered most from emotional exhaustion.

Such statistical methods were not always enlightening because of the difficulty of framing appropriate questions. Difficulties had been found in such questionnaries because of the perception that clergy had of the desires of lay people. Appraisal of clergy could be constructive but had dangers because of the hierarchical structure. Appropriate selection and training of the appraisers was felt to be vital. No single formula for support systems would be effective in every situation.

Paul Beetham

YOUTH

The Rev. Dr. William Kay led a discussion with about two dozen people on the subject of Youth. Dr. Kay and the Rev. Dr. Leslie Francis have recently published a book (Teenage Religion and Values, published by gracewing) on the results of a survey of teenage attitudes to religion and morality. Dr. Kay talked about the nature of the survey and what it had discovered. His talk was peppered with questions from his hearers.

The survey had been addressed to boys and girls at school in the 13 to 15 age group, a period before the pressures of important exams had arrived, but suitably old to show observable trends due to age changes. The survey's results were drawn from 13,065 children in 65 different schools. Each child was given a booklet of questions which took about an hour to complete. They were filled in anonymously. There were 90 multiple choice questions, 128 Likert items (i.e. a statement with five possible responses), 24 personality items, and a further 70 questions for churchgoers only. The big sample was needed in order to make sub-groups big enough to be worth comparing. There were too few Jews, Mormons or Muslims to merit a separate sample, so answers from children from those backgrounds were not included in the 13,065 whose responses were taken into account.

Dr. Kay gave examples of the survey's results in the following sections.

Belonging, Believing and Practising

In some subjects the survey was taken as a whole -

Belief in God:
- 44% were theist
- 33% were agnostic
- 23% were atheist

Church attendance:
- 16% regularly (monthly)
- 38% occasional
- 46% never

In other subjects figures were subdivided between
1. those who did not believe in God. (A)
2. those who believed but did not attend Church. (B)
3. those who believed and did attend Church. (C)

In Group (B)
    44% never pray
    69% never read the Bible
    92% never say grace at meals
    70% believe Jesus is the son of God
    51% believe Jesus really rose from the dead
    52% believe in life after death
    26% are creationist (take Genesis 1 literally)

In Group (C)
    5% never pray
    17% never read the Bible
    52% never say grace at meals
    94% believe Jesus is the son of God
    85% believe Jesus really rose from the dead
    61% believe in life after death
    42% are creationist

In Group (C)
    8% pray from time to time(!)

Drugs (including alcohol and tobacco

The percentages relate to children who agree with the following statements:

	Group (A)	Group (B)	Group (C)
It is wrong to become drunk	22%	23%	34%
It is wrong to smoke	41%	45%	56%
It is wrong to use marijuana	52%	64%	69%
It is wrong to us heroin	74%	82%	88%
It is wrong to sniff glue	78%	83%	86%

Girls are more inclined than boys to be traditional, <u>except</u> with smoking.

These figures give grounds for believing that belief in God (even in Group B) is the beginning of a moral framework.

Sexual Morality

These percentages too relate to agreement with the following statements:

	Group (A)	Group (B)	Group (C)
Sex outside marriage is wrong	10%	15%	30%
Divorce is wrong	20%	23%	30%
Homosexuality is wrong	44%	44%	42%
Contraception is wrong	6%	7%	6%
Abortion is wrong	27%	45%	41%

Taking the survey as a whole 24% said that under-age sex is wrong, but 76% implied that it was not.

Roman Catholics tend to disagree with their Church's official teaching about contraception but to agree with it about abortion. Contrary to the impression given by the media, only 1% or less of adult males have practised homosexuality, and an even smaller percentage of adult females have practised lesbianism.

Further Issues

1. Believers who go to Church tend to be much more concerned than others about social issues (e.g. third world poverty,

pollution, environment), and are much more willing to do something about them.
2. When they are in trouble, all children in this age group are more likely to go for advice to their mother or doctor than to go to their father, social worker or clergy. Girls are much more likely than boys to 'network' their problems, i.e. discuss intimately with girl friends.
3. How hopeful are young people? For about one third, life is rosy in terms of education, home, job prospects and so on, and they are hopeful. About one tenth are totally alienated from home, school, politics and church, and they play truant, dabble in drugs and graffiti, and are without hope. The rest are somewhere in the middle.

APPENDIX

MEDITATION
A SHORT WORD MAP

WHO?
For all, not just a special, religious, gifted, serious group: for all ages, women, men, children...............

WHY?
An age-old, world-wide tradition bringing healing, harmony, stillness, balance, love, joy, peace.
A two-way channel between you, your God, others, our environment; Simple, proven profound.
Relates to whole person, spirit, mind, feelings, will, body, relationships
Goes to the heart, through the head but then on.
Good for blood pressure, muscles ....
Develops your unlimited potential, increasing efficiency and effectiveness, calming your mind, promoting positive feelings.

WHAT?
About loving, giving and receiving. Learning to love self, your God, others and to receive the wonderful, unending stream of love directed towards you. Knowing you are loved, unconditionally. Plugging in to the life of God, Father, Son and Holy Spirit. Exploring inner space, the meaning of lif/God. Praying, words and beyond words. Paradox, e.g. the silent music of love. Experience, within and beyond all experiences, in the end indescribable.

VISUALISATION, focusing, centring, concentrating, paying attention, e.g. 'seeing' a candle, imagining a peaceful, beautiful place; focusing solely on the winning tape and seeing you break it.

REFLECTION; e.g. letting a word such as love sink into you; sucking a paradox such as nothing matters, everything matters.

CONTEMPLATION; from head to heart, thought to stillness, noise to silence, relaxation to alert awareness/openness of being, communication to communion.

HOW?
There are no quick fixes, *no magic!* It is a life-long, eternal way. But every journey has a start. You will need Trust, Courage, Commitment, Discipline, Perseverance for an essentially Simple journey.

TECHNIQUE. Important as a means to an end; a hi-fi system is for experiencing sound! Nothing is absolutely right for everyone, everywhere. What is right is what is right for you. But have the humility to learn from the vast store of experience and those many others who are well down the way. Remember what may feel awkward at the start, with persistence may be right for you.

SOME BASICS
Find a quiet space as possible, though you can meditate in a thunderstorm or a traffic jam.

Sit on a chair or the floor with your back straight, enabling energy flow. But if lying on the floor does it for you, fine; though remember meditation is more than relaxation. Close your eyes if it helps you.

Rest your hands in your lap or on your knees. Tell yourself to relax. Relax your muscles, especially in your neck and shoulders.

Repeat three times, 'Be still and know that I am God'.

Breathe from your stomach, through your nose, gently slowly. Focus on your breathing. As you breath out, start to say your mantra, Ma-ra-na-tha, rhythmically. It means in Aramaic 'Our Lord comes' though the meaning is of lesser importance. If you are more comfortable with another word, e.g. love, om, then use it. The purpose of the mantra/little word is to lead to the stillness beyond words. Resist the urge to scratch your leg! Your mind is probably not used to being still, doesn't like it and distracting thoughts will come. Say to yourself 'How interesting', quietly tell them to go and return to your breathing/mantra. Be patient with, kind to yourself. You have a life/eternity to learn to be still. Sometimes you will feel great, sometimes not so great, sometimes not much. Fine! Just carry on. You will know the peace which passes understanding. There are no performance indicators!

It is best to meditate twice a day for 20/30 minutes. If for a variety of reasons you cannot manage this, do what you can, where/when you can. Something is better than nothing. But remember to examine carefully and honestly your priorities and life-style in terms of time/purpose. We can nearly always do most of what we really want to do. There is nothing more important in the universe than meditating!

It is a great help to be part of a Meditation Group if possible. It enables exchange, learning/teaching, supporting, guiding, encouraging. A Group meets every Thursday at Mold Methodist Church, Wrexham Street, 7.30 to 8.45 p.m. It is part of an international network. There may be a Group near you. Or you could perhaps start a Group!

For more information contact Neville Stewart at:

5 Church Meadow, Rhydymwyn, Mold, Clwyd, CH7 5HX Tel. 01352 741492

Reading List

In addition to books written by the contributors to the Consultation, the following may be of interest to those wishing to undertake further study. Lists have been provided by Professor David Booth, Alex Darlington, Roy Edwards and Bertie Everard.

Barry, R (1993) *A Theory of Almost Everything: A Scientific and Religious Quest for Ultimate Answers*, Oneworld Publications.

Capra, F (1993) *The Turning Point: Science, Society and the Rising Culture*, Flamingo.

Cosgrove, M.P. and Mallory, J.D. (1977) *Mental Health: a Christian Approach*, Paternoster Press.

Darling, H.W. (1970) *Man in His Right Mind*, Paternoster Press.

Evans, C.S. (1979) *Preserving the Person*, Intervarsity Press.

Fowler, J.W. (1981) *Stages of Faith: The Psychology of Human Development and the Quest for Meaning*, Harper & Row.

Goodwin, R. (1976) *Stress at Work*, Chester House Publications.

Guinness, O (1973) *The Dust of Death*, Intervarsity Press.

Harrison, R. (1987) *Organisational Culture and Quality of Service: A Strategy for Releasing Love in the Workplace*, Association for Management Education and Development.

Hay, D. (1990) *Religious Experience Today: Studying the Facts*, Mowbray.

Hurding, R.F. (1985) *Roots and Shoots: a Guide to Counselling and Psychotherapy*, Hodder and & Stoughton.

Hurding, F.R. (1992) *The Bible and Counselling*, Hodder & Stoughton.

Jacobs, M., *Towards the Fullness of Christ* [on pastoral care and Christian maturity].

Jeeves, M.A. (1976) *Psychology and Christianity: the View Both Ways*, Intervarsity Press.

Jeeves, M.A. (Ed.) (1984) *Behavioural Sciences: a Christian Perspective*, Intervarsity Press.

Knudson, *Sociology: the Encounter of Christianity with Secular Science*, Institute of Christian Studies.

McGrath, A. & J. (1992) *The Dilemma of Self-esteem*, Crossway

Myers, D.G. (1978) *The Human Puzzle: Psychological Research and Christian Belief*, Harper & Row.

Myers, D.G. (1983) *The Pursuit of Happiness: Who is Happy - and Why*, Harper/Collins Aquarian.

Myers, D.G. and Jeeves, M. (1991) *Psychology through the Eyes of Faith*, Apollos

Olthuis, *Straddling the Boundaries between Theology and Psychology: The Faith-Feeling Interface*, Institute of Christian Studies.

Pearson, A. (1994) *Growing through Loss and Grief: A Counsellor's Guide*, Marshall Pickering.

Plunkett, D. (1990) *Secular and Spiritual Values: Grounds for Hope in Education*, Routledge.

RSA Templeton Lectures (1993) *Explorations in Science and Theology*, Royal Society of Arts.

van Leeuwen, M.S. (1985) *The Person in Psychology*, Intervarsity Press.

van Leeuwen, M.S., *The Behaviourist Bandwagon and the Body of Christ*, Institute of Christian Studies.

Ward, K., *Defending the Soul*, Oneworld Publications.

Watson, W. (1987) *Education and Belief*, Blackwell.

Consciousness and transcendental Reality
David R. Copestake

Experiences of a religious, spiritual or transcendental nature have often been claimed to provide evidence of a transcendental reality or God. Those who have the experiences are usually utterly convinced, but the sceptics may doubt. Richard Dawkins is one such sceptic. He confesses that he has had overwhelming experiences of wonder and joy in nature, especially in a tropical rain forest, but assigns all 'religious' feelings and experiences to 'virtual reality stimulating machinery in the brain'. He says, "It would be child's play for that virtual reality software to knock up a still, small voice in your head talking to you. So I'm not in the least impressed with somebody saying 'God talked to me', or 'I saw a vision of the Virgin Mary'". [1]
Let us in thinking about this first consider ordinary human consciousness. This is still much of a mystery and its origins are obscure. Perhaps the story of Adam and Eve and the tree of knowledge in Genesis is really a mythical account of the dawning of self-consciousness in human life. One thing is clear and that is that consciousness depends on the coming into existence of certain forms of very complex organisations of matter. These are nervous systems and brains which have become more and more complex in the evolutionary development. This increasing complexity is manifest in biological development as an increasing sensitivity to changes in the environment. The more adept at recording, analysing and making reliable predictions from information about its environment, the better chance an organism will have of surviving. There is in this development what can be called a propensity for an increase in information-processing ability.
Konrad Lorenz, the ethologist, in the early 1940's made the point that unless an organism's processing of incoming information was

---

[1] The Daily Telegraph 31.8.92

broadly trustworthy, it would not have survived and evolved by natural selection. In order to survive it has to be able to ascertain sufficiently accurately what the surrounding world is really like. Thus creatures have evolved eyes because there is something out there for the eye to see that provides significant information for survival.

We can say then that ordinary consciousness gives moderately correct (that is correct enough) information about the outside reality. Organisms that could not do this would be weeded out by natural selection because they could not have reproduced so quickly.

Turning to the emergence of the religious consciousness or spiritual and transcendent awareness, it has been believed for many years that this factor has been an aid to human survival. This was shown by R.R. Marett, the Oxford anthropologist in his studies of primitive societies and religion. Marett believed that religious feelings included a more important aspect than magic or animism as emphasised by Frazer and Tyler. This was the recognition of a benign power beyond themselves and was basically a feeling of power beyond the self giving strength and encouragement. This had survival value and so became an evolutionary factor in human behaviour.[1]

More recently the well known American psychologist Donald T. Campbell in discussing social evolution, argued that individual selfish tendencies which biological evolution continued to select for ('selfish' here in the sense of the 'selfish' gene, protecting one's own genetic kin) had been countered principally by religion. As people lived for a transcendent God's purposes, the selfish urges of the individual were overcome, thus enabling humanity to survive and flourish.[2]

---

[1] 1932, Faith Hope and Charity in Primitive Religion, OUP

[2] See Zygon 11, 1976, pp. 167-208.

This suggests two things; first, that these social values enshrined in religious moral codes and imprinted in ethical attitudes, are part of the realities with which we humans have to deal and take account of or otherwise die out. Second, can the well documented experiences of a 'transcendental reality' and the religious consciousness which many people steel feel today, alone out of all human experiences, have no contact with any reality essential for human survival and flourishing? Surely these experiences and the cumulative wisdom of the religious traditions point together to a level of human consciousness whereby there is an awareness of an all-encompassing Reality that transcends all, and yet is imminent in all existence. This Reality is essential for human survival and flourishing, is what people call God, and relates to the religious consciousness just as the environment relates to ordinary consciousness.[1]

---

[1] I am indebted to Dr. Arthur Peacocke's Alister Hardy Memorial Lecture, 1989 for many of the ideas in this issue.

Printing by
Jiffy Print Limited
9 King Street, Luton, Bedfordshire LU1 2DW
Great Britain